Faithful Prepping Security in Spirit

M.Ray Davis

Published by Dragon Bear Publishing, LLC, 2025.

While every precaution has been taken in the preparation of this book, the publisher assumes no responsibility for errors or omissions, or for damages resulting from the use of the information contained herein.

FAITHFUL PREPPING SECURITY IN SPIRIT

First edition. December 1, 2025.

Copyright © 2025 M.Ray Davis.

ISBN: 979-8990677418

Written by M.Ray Davis.

This book is dedicated to all who have chosen to become Preparedness Leaders in thier own churches.

Introduction: Preparedness as a Ministry of Hope

Disaster preparedness isn't just about stockpiling supplies or drawing up emergency plans. For the church, it can be one of the most practical and Spirit-led ministries we offer to our people and our community. Why? Because it weaves together two core values of the Christian life: self-reliance rooted in stewardship and community rooted in love.

The church has always been more than a building. It is our spiritual home—a place of worship, of comfort, and of fellowship. And when crisis strikes, those very things become lifelines. Fellowship lifts morale when fear sets in. Prayer sustains weary hearts. A familiar sanctuary becomes not just a place of worship but a place of refuge.

Preparedness, then, is not about fear of "what if." It is about ensuring that the light of Christ continues to shine, even when the power grid does not. It is about making sure that worship, prayer, and care can go on uninterrupted when the world outside seems shaken.

Why Churches Should Be Ready

When disaster hits, people don't usually run to city hall or search for the closest government office. More often than not, they head for the nearest church. Why? Because the church is already familiar. It's where they've prayed, where they've gathered, where they've found comfort in times past. The church is a place of hope.

That's why preparedness is not just a good idea for the church — it's part of our ministry. When storms rage, people will look to the church for strength. We may not be the Red Cross, but we can be a place of safety and encouragement. Just by being present — with open doors, warm lights, and helping hands — the church can give courage to those who feel like giving up.

We also know the faces of those most likely to be forgotten in a crisis. The elderly, the homebound, the single parent, the family without transportation — they are already part of our congregations and communities. Churches are uniquely positioned to see them, to check on them, and to serve them when others may not.

And while food and water are vital, so is peace of mind. In moments of fear and grief, pastors, leaders, and fellow believers can speak words no agency ever could: prayer that calms the heart, Scripture that restores hope, and encouragement that strengthens the soul.

Churches are also natural centers of organization. We know how to come together for potlucks, mission drives, and service projects. In the same way, we can rally volunteers, distribute supplies, or even just offer a warm meal and a place to recharge a phone.

Most importantly, preparedness allows the work of the church to continue. Worship, prayer, and care do not need to stop because the power is out or the storm has passed through. With a plan in place, the life of the church continues, bearing witness that the gospel never shuts down.

When a congregation takes preparedness seriously, it sends a message: "We are here for you — no matter what." That kind of faithfulness builds trust, strengthens resilience, and testifies to God's steady hand in the storm.

What Church Preparedness Looks Like

Preparedness isn't complicated or mysterious. It begins by looking honestly at the risks in our community — floods, tornadoes, hurricanes, or wildfires — and asking, "What can we do now to be ready?" From there, a plan is developed so that when trouble comes, no one is left scrambling. Roles are assigned, communication methods are clear, and evacuation routes are understood.

Supplies are gathered, not in fear, but in wisdom — a modest store of water, food, first aid, and radios that could transform the church into a safe haven when the community needs it most. Volunteers are trained so that when the moment comes, the skills God has already placed in the congregation — medical knowledge, carpentry, counseling, communication — can be put into action.

And preparedness extends beyond the church walls. Partnering with local emergency services and other congregations multiplies our reach.

Together, we can serve more people and offer a united witness of God's love in action.

A Call to Purpose

By the end of this journey, you won't just have a plan on paper. You'll carry a renewed sense of purpose. Preparedness will no longer feel like a side project — it will feel like ministry. It will feel like love for God and love for neighbor put into action in the hardest of times.

Every step toward preparedness is a step toward a stronger body of Christ. Every gallon of water stored, every volunteer trained, every plan practiced is one more way we say to the world: "The church is here, and the church is ready."

So let us take these steps with hope and determination. A prepared church is not just a safe church — it is a light in the darkness, a sanctuary of resilience, and a testimony of God's love when people need it most.

Chapter 1

The Emergency Management Cycle — A Framework for a Faithful Response

When we talk about disaster preparedness, it's easy to feel overwhelmed. Where do we even begin? The truth is, emergency management follows a simple rhythm called the Disaster Management Cycle. Think of it as a roadmap that helps us not just react when crisis comes, but prepare, respond, and recover in a way that reflects both wisdom and faith.

The cycle has four main parts.

Mitigation is all about reducing the impact before it happens. Just like Noah built the ark before the flood, we take steps now to minimize loss of life and damage when storms come.

Preparedness is where we plan, train, and gather resources. In this stage, we ask: what has God already placed in our hands, and how can we use it wisely?

Response is action in the moment. It's when we open our doors, check on our people, and do what needs to be done to protect life and provide care.

Recovery is about rebuilding, restoring, and healing after the storm has passed. It's when the church can become a beacon of hope in the long journey back to normal.

Understanding this cycle helps us see that preparedness is not just reactionary — it's proactive, ongoing, and deeply tied to our calling as God's people.

Knowing Your Risks

Every congregation faces different challenges. A church in California may not worry about tornadoes, but earthquakes and wildfires are always in the back of their minds. A church in Iowa might not think about hurricanes, but they know how quickly floods and twisters can form. Preparedness begins with honesty: What are the real risks in our area, and how can we be ready for them?

This is not just about identifying what could go wrong. It's about planning ahead to reduce the impact when those situations inevitably come. In this chapter, we'll look at practical steps for evaluating your church building, understanding the risks tied to your ministries and events, and developing plans that reflect the unique needs of your congregation.

Evaluating the Church Building

Our buildings are more than walls and roofs; they're spiritual homes. But we can't assume they are automatically safe. Older churches may have wiring that isn't up to code, exits that are too narrow, or structures that aren't built to handle today's storms. Regular inspections — done by professionals — can reveal weaknesses before they become tragedies. Think of it as stewardship: caring for the physical house of worship so it continues to be a place of refuge.

Considering Events and Attendance

Churches aren't one-size-fits-all in their activities. A Wednesday night prayer group looks very different from a wedding with 400 guests or a youth retreat packed with energy. Each of these gatherings carries different risks. Overcrowding, blocked exits, or lack of supervision can all create dangerous situations. Preparing for them doesn't mean living in fear; it means using wisdom so that each person who walks through our doors is safe.

Ensuring Resources and Training

Preparedness is not just about stuff — it's about people knowing how to use it. A first aid kit doesn't save lives unless someone knows where it is and how to use it. Fire exits don't help unless people know the route. That's why part of preparedness is making sure supplies are stocked and training is regular. Practice drills may feel awkward at first, but they build confidence and create a culture of safety in the church.

Involving the Whole Congregation

The church is a body, not a building. Preparedness works best when everyone plays a part. Maybe one member is a nurse, another is a carpenter, another knows radio communications. By involving the congregation in planning and drills, we not only share the load but also foster a spirit of unity. Preparing together reminds us: we are responsible for one another.

Learning From the Past

Every community has stories of storms, power outages, or near-misses. Some are written down in reports; others are remembered by the oldest members of the church. Both matter. Looking at history gives us perspective on what might happen again. If floods rise every spring or the power goes out every few years, that pattern should guide our planning. God often uses memory to teach us how to prepare for the future.

Working With Local Emergency Services

Preparedness doesn't mean going it alone. Local fire, police, and medical services are not competitors — they are partners. Building relationships with them ahead of time helps the church know what to expect and how to cooperate. It also allows them to know us, our building, and our unique needs. Inviting them to lead workshops or run drills with our volunteers builds trust and ensures smoother coordination when real emergencies strike.

Creating, Updating, and Practicing the Plan

A plan is only as good as the last time it was updated. Congregations grow, buildings change, and risks evolve. A preparedness plan is a living document, not a one-time project. Establishing a safety committee that reviews and revises the plan keeps it current. Practicing the plan through drills and small-scale scenarios ensures that when the real thing happens, people know what to do.

Final Thoughts

Preparedness isn't about expecting the worst — it's about being faithful stewards of what God has given us. The Emergency Management Cycle reminds us that disasters aren't one-time events; they are seasons we move through: preparing, responding, recovering, and learning as we go.

When a church embraces preparedness, it transforms from being a vulnerable target into a resilient sanctuary. It becomes a place not only of worship but of safety, stability, and light in the midst of crisis.

Remember, safety is not a one-time task. It is an ongoing ministry. By involving the congregation, training volunteers, partnering with local responders, and reviewing plans regularly, we create a culture where preparedness is woven into the life of the church.

And when the day comes — as it surely will — that disaster strikes, we will not be caught off guard. We will be ready to respond, ready to serve, and ready to shine as a testimony of God's steady hand in the storm.

Chapter 2

Creating a Tailored Disaster Response Plan
Devotional Reflection: The Church as a Refuge
"God is our refuge and strength, an ever-present help in trouble." —Psalm 46:1

All throughout Scripture, God reveals Himself as a place of safety. In the storms of life, He is our rock. In the chaos of battle, He is our shield. In the wilderness, He is our shelter. When fear threatens to overwhelm, He reminds us that His presence is steady, unshakable, and sure.

The church, as His body, is called to reflect that same heart of refuge. Our buildings may not be fortresses, but they are houses of prayer. Our members may not be first responders by profession, but we are called to respond with love, wisdom, and readiness. When crisis comes—whether it's a storm, a fire, or an unforeseen emergency—the church has the opportunity to become a living signpost of God's care: calm in the chaos, light in the darkness, and community in the loneliness.

Every church is different. Each congregation has its own unique mix of people, strengths, challenges, and resources. That's why disaster response plans should never be "one-size-fits-all." A tailored plan is essential because it makes sure every member of the body is seen, valued, and protected. When the church prepares in a way that reflects its own people, it doesn't just increase safety—it strengthens fellowship, unity, and witness.

Building a Disaster Response Committee

The first step is bringing together a team that represents the heart and diversity of the church. This isn't just about filling seats on a committee—it's about drawing on the gifts and experiences God has already placed in the congregation. Imagine the wisdom of a nurse who knows what medical supplies are essential, combined with the insight of someone who has lived through a disaster and knows what it feels like when everything falls apart. Add in the skills of a logistics-minded member who can organize supplies, and a communicator who can keep messages clear and calm, and suddenly the church is equipped with a powerhouse of experience and compassion.

Forming this kind of team sends a powerful message: preparedness is not the work of one or two leaders; it is the shared responsibility of the whole body of Christ. As Paul reminds us in 1 Corinthians 12, every part matters. And when every part works together, the whole body is stronger.

For the committee to succeed, roles need to be clearly defined. When disaster strikes, there's no time for confusion. Each member should know exactly what they are responsible for and how their role fits into the bigger picture. One may handle communication, another supplies, another medical needs, and another volunteer coordination. Clear responsibilities not only prevent overlap but also build confidence that nothing will fall through the cracks.

And don't overlook the power of encouragement and recognition. Formally acknowledging the committee's mission—whether from the pulpit, in the bulletin, or at a special commissioning—reminds everyone this work is not just logistics. It is ministry.

Keeping the Team Ready

Even the best plan will gather dust if it isn't practiced. That's why regular communication, training, and drills are so important. Meetings keep everyone on the same page, but they also build trust. A team that talks often is a team that learns to rely on each other. Training sessions turn good intentions into muscle memory. The more you practice evacuation routes, first aid, or communication protocols, the more natural they become. In a real crisis, those practiced skills could save lives.

Drills also bring the congregation into the process. When members practice evacuation together or run through a storm shelter plan, they move from being passive bystanders to active participants in their own safety. It shifts preparedness from "the committee's job" to "our shared responsibility."

Communication That Reaches Everyone

In any crisis, information is as vital as food and water. A well-crafted disaster plan must include communication strategies that keep everyone connected, calm, and informed. That means going beyond a single method. Phone calls, text alerts, social media posts, emails, and even radios may all play a role. Different people use different tools, so multiple channels ensure no one is left in the dark.

Communication also changes depending on the stage of the crisis. Before an incident, updates might include preparedness reminders. During the incident, communication should focus on safety instructions and real-time updates. Afterward, messages shift toward support, recovery, and encouragement. Planning for each stage ensures no moment is wasted.

And let's not forget those who face extra challenges. Some may not have smartphones. Others may need messages in another language, larger print, or simplified formats. Tailoring communication to reach vulnerable members reflects the heart of Christ—who always sought out those most likely to be overlooked.

Caring for the Vulnerable

A truly Christian disaster plan cannot ignore the needs of the most vulnerable. The elderly, the disabled, the chronically ill, single parents, and those without transportation all need extra support when a crisis hits. To overlook them would not only weaken the plan but also contradict the very mission of the church.

That's why individualized planning matters. Confidential surveys, one-on-one conversations, or family interviews can help identify who needs extra help and how best to provide it. Maybe it's arranging transport for someone with mobility challenges, ensuring a steady supply of medication, or pairing a vulnerable member with a "safety buddy" during evacuations.

This is where the church can truly shine. While agencies may overlook those on the margins, the church is called to step in. As Galatians 6:2 reminds us, "Carry each other's burdens, and in this way you will fulfill the law of Christ."

Partnering Beyond the Church

Preparedness doesn't happen in a bubble. Partnering with local fire departments, EMS, hospitals, and emergency managers opens the door to resources, training, and wisdom that the church may not have on its own. Inviting first responders to lead workshops or participate in joint drills strengthens not only the plan but also the bonds between the church and its wider community.

When responders know your building, your people, and your plan, they can help more effectively. And when your church is prepared, it can in turn lighten their load during a disaster. It's a partnership that honors God by working together for the good of all.

Bringing It All Together

By the end of this process, what you have is more than a document on paper. You have a living plan rooted in the gifts of your people, the wisdom of experience, and the compassion of Christ. You have communication systems that keep fear from spreading faster than the crisis itself. You have strategies that make sure no one—especially the vulnerable—is forgotten. And you have partnerships that connect your church to the broader community of care.

This isn't just about being safe. It's about being faithful. A tailored disaster response plan reflects the truth that the church is not a building—it's a body. And when disaster strikes, that body is ready to move as one: calm, prepared, and full of the love of Christ.

Chapter 3

Training and Equipping Church Members for Emergency Preparedness

Training and equipping church members for emergency preparedness is key to building a community that can respond effectively when it matters most. The ability to handle situations like medical emergencies, fires, or natural disasters can greatly influence the outcome and safety of everyone involved. It's not just about having the skills but also making sure these skills are up-to-date and practiced regularly. This chapter focuses on how, by preparing the congregation with the right tools, knowledge, and mentality, churches can create an environment of safety and readiness. By fostering this kind of culture, not only does personal safety improve, but so does the resilience and interconnectedness of the community as a whole.

In this chapter, we will explore various ways churches can organize training sessions for their members, focusing particularly on first aid and CPR workshops. These sessions provide crucial hands-on experience under professional guidance, ensuring that participants learn practical application along with theoretical knowledge. Furthermore, we'll look at how interactive elements such as role-playing scenarios can make these sessions more engaging and memorable. Beyond skill acquisition, continuous learning through refresher courses ensures proficiency remains high. Regular updates are vital to staying informed about new techniques or changes in protocol. Moreover, establishing a culture of readiness within a church involves integrating emergency preparedness into its core values, including promoting collaborative efforts during sermons and creating mentorship opportunities among experienced and new members alike. Finally, this chapter addresses the importance of drills and personalized emergency plans, which further strengthen the collective readiness of church members, making preparedness a shared responsibility across the entire community.

Organizing First Aid and CPR Workshops

Equipping congregation members with critical first aid and CPR skills is a vital component in fostering a secure and prepared community. The ability to respond effectively in emergencies not only ensures personal safety but also provides immediate assistance to others in need, potentially saving lives.

To achieve this, churches can benefit by engaging certified trainers who bring expertise and current knowledge. Certified trainers are essential because they provide accurate, up-to-date information on medical practices that may have changed over time due to advances in healthcare. Their proficiency and training enable them to convey essential life-saving techniques through hands-on experience, allowing participants to practice under professional guidance. This approach ensures that the members are not only learning theoretically but also understanding the practical application of these skills.

Moreover, training sessions should be designed to be interactive and engaging, incorporating role-playing scenarios to reinforce the skills taught. By simulating real-life emergency situations, participants can better grasp how to handle stress and execute what they've learned. For instance, role-playing a situation where someone is having a heart attack allows the trainees to visualize steps like assessing the scene for safety, calling for help, performing CPR, and using an AED if available. These simulations promote active learning and make the sessions more enjoyable and memorable.

Continuous learning is key to maintaining proficiency in these crucial skills. Regular updates and refresher courses ensure that the congregation remains well-informed about any changes or new techniques in first aid and CPR. Just as one might renew a driving license after several years, refreshing these skills is necessary to prevent complacency and boost confidence. Additionally, offering these refresher courses at convenient times can motivate more members to participate regularly, thereby enhancing the collective readiness of the church community.

Establishing a culture of readiness within the church is another pivotal element. When the leaders and members both value and engage seriously with emergency preparedness training, it fosters a community where everyone feels responsible for one another's safety. Church leaders can play a crucial role here by promoting these programs during sermons or community meetings, emphasizing the importance of being prepared not just for oneself, but as a means of serving others in times of crisis.

Encouraging stories and testimonies from those who've successfully used their training to make a difference can also inspire other members to take part. Whether it's helping a neighbor who fell or assisting during a community event, these narratives can underscore the real-world impact of the training. Plus, pairing experienced members with newcomers can create mentorship opportunities, strengthening bonds and reinforcing a collaborative culture of preparedness.

Implementation of regular evacuation drills and personal emergency plans, although addressed separately in different subpoints, complements the readiness culture by providing structure and context to the skills learned. Seeing how effective CPR and first aid fit into broader emergency response strategies can drive home the relevance and urgency of mastering these skills. It also ensures that congregants understand their roles within larger safety protocols, which can be critical when seconds count in an actual emergency.

Finally, fostering an environment of mutual respect and encouragement ensures that all members, regardless of age or ability, feel welcome and valued in these learning experiences. Tailoring programs to accommodate diverse needs and ensuring accessibility for those with disabilities or unique challenges further reflects the inclusive spirit of the church. Leaders can solicit feedback from participants to continually improve the effectiveness and inclusivity of the training sessions.

Implementing Regular Evacuation Drills

In any emergency, having a clear and efficient evacuation plan is crucial for ensuring the safety of everyone involved. The cornerstone of an effective evacuation strategy lies in identifying all available exits and escape routes. It's essential to consider different types of emergencies that might arise, such as fires, earthquakes, or severe weather conditions. Each scenario may require a unique route or different considerations for safe evacuation. By mapping out multiple paths, church members can be prepared to safely navigate their way to safety, regardless of the situation at hand.

Picture this: the church is packed on a Sunday morning, and suddenly a fire alarm goes off. Panic could easily spread among the congregation if they aren't familiar with the exits. By using clearly marked signs and regular walkthroughs, everyone present would know exactly where to go. This familiarity can significantly reduce anxiety and confusion during actual events.

Conducting consistent and varied drills is another essential part of preparing church members for potential emergencies. Drills serve as practical exercises that help individuals react instinctively rather than hesitantly. To break the monotony and enhance learning, these drills should differ in nature—sometimes simulating a fire, other times an intruder situation or a natural disaster. Through variety, participants can develop a well-rounded understanding of how to respond in different contexts.

Imagine staging a mock drill with different scenarios that lead congregants through various exit routes. By scheduling periodic training, you not only reinforce these crucial skills but also keep the process engaging and fresh. Participants are more likely to retain what they've learned when they're periodically revisiting these key techniques. This keeps everyone on their toes and ready for anything life throws their way.

After each drill, gathering feedback is vital. The insights gained from participants can highlight areas needing improvement or reveal overlooked aspects of the plan. For instance, a practice run might expose bottlenecks in high-traffic areas or difficulties faced by individuals with mobility challenges. Gathering this input should be seen as an opportunity to refine the plans continually. Encourage open discussions post-drill, allowing everyone to voice observations and suggestions.

Consistent feedback loops ensure the plan evolves and adapts to new findings, making it stronger with time. Once changes are made, inform the entire congregation of updates so everyone remains aware and informed. The continuous cycle of practice, feedback, and improvement builds a resilient and responsive community.

Inclusivity is another vital element in developing a comprehensive evacuation plan. Engaging diverse demographics within the church ensures that the safety strategy accounts for everyone's needs. Consider the specific requirements of children, elderly members, and those with disabilities. These groups may need additional assistance or alternative routes for a safe evacuation.

Involving these groups in the planning process fosters a sense of belonging and ensures their voices are heard. Demonstrating sensitivity to individual needs showcases the church's commitment to everyone's well-being. Additionally, you might include multilingual signage or provide translation services during training sessions to accommodate non-English speakers, ensuring everyone comprehensively understands the procedures.

To create an atmosphere of security, it's important to maintain open communication channels. Encouraging congregants to share their concerns about evacuation plans or suggest improvements can enhance the preparation process. When everyone feels heard and valued, they are more likely to take the initiative seriously and engage fully in the effort.

As church leaders, your dedication to keeping the community safe becomes evident through these inclusive efforts, and it sends a message of unity. Working together towards a common goal strengthens both the church's bond and its ability to handle emergencies effectively.

Remember, the ultimate aim is to cultivate a culture of preparedness where every person knows precisely what to do in an emergency. With frequent practice and continual refinement, members gain confidence, knowing they can rely on themselves and each other when it matters most. This proactive approach doesn't just prepare individuals for emergencies; it reinforces a collective spirit of readiness that benefits the entire community.

Promoting Individual Preparedness Plans

Fostering a sense of personal responsibility in emergency preparedness is crucial for church members to effectively protect themselves and their families. By taking ownership of preparing for emergencies, individuals not only ensure their safety but also contribute to the resilience of the entire community. A great starting point is providing resources like checklists and guides. These tools can serve as practical aids for creating personalized emergency plans that cater to each family's specific needs and circumstances.

Developing these plans can feel overwhelming at first, but using well-structured checklists simplifies the process. These lists should cover basic necessities such as food, water, medical supplies, and communication devices. Supplementing checklists with detailed guides enhances preparedness by offering step-by-step instructions on executing these plans effectively during an emergency situation. Encourage church leaders to distribute these materials in meetings or via digital platforms so they're easily accessible to everyone.

Involving families in planning efforts is another vital aspect. When families plan together, they build stronger bonds and improve their ability to respond collectively in times of crisis. Encouraging every family member, regardless of age, to participate fosters a team spirit and ensures that everyone knows their role in an emergency. For example, children can be taught simple tasks like recognizing alarm signals or knowing safe meeting points. This communal approach not only equips them to deal with potential emergencies but also strengthens the overall resilience of the church community.

Addressing the unique needs of vulnerable members is essential in emergency preparedness. Vulnerable members include seniors, people with disabilities, or those with chronic health conditions, and they might require special assistance in creating and executing their emergency plans. Tailored support is fundamental to ensuring that these individuals are not left behind when emergencies occur. Church leaders can organize workshops that address these specific needs, inviting healthcare professionals or social workers to provide expert advice. Additionally, buddy systems can be established where able-bodied congregants commit to checking on and assisting their vulnerable peers.

Communication plays a key role in fostering mutual aid and cooperation among church members. Open lines of communication encourage congregants to share resources, knowledge, and support with one another. Regularly scheduled meetings or group discussions on emergency preparedness can serve as forums for sharing ideas and strategies. It's important to highlight the benefits of staying connected during crises, such as being informed about the latest developments or mobilizing resources quickly.

Congregants should be encouraged to exchange contact information and form small support groups within the community. These groups can serve multiple purposes; they can act as accountability partners, motivators, and immediate responders during an emergency. Promoting a culture of collective responsibility helps build trust and unity, which are critical components not just for emergency preparedness but for the overall strength of the church community.

While it's important to focus on immediate family needs, looking beyond personal plans can significantly enhance the preparedness level. Establishing a library of books, videos, and online courses related to first aid and CPR can be incredibly useful. Church leaders can guide members in accessing these resources, ensuring they are equipped with the necessary skills to handle medical emergencies before professional help arrives.

Engaging every demographic helps ensure that no one is overlooked, making the community's emergency preparedness efforts comprehensive. Diverse perspectives from different age groups and backgrounds enrich the planning process. By involving youth groups, women's ministries, and senior circles in discussions, churches can generate inclusive strategies tailored to varied needs.

Conducting evacuation drills is a critical exercise that every church should prioritize to ensure the safety and preparedness of its congregation members. Routine drills familiar to escape routes and procedures reduce panic and increase efficiency when real emergencies strike. After each drill, gathering feedback can uncover areas needing improvement, creating opportunities for continuous refinement of emergency plans.

Certification and Access to Professionals

When it comes to preparing church members for emergencies, credibility is an essential element that cannot be overlooked. This is where the role of certification becomes significant. Certification programs do more than just equip individuals with knowledge; they instill confidence and underscore the importance of being prepared. Knowing that training is certified reassures participants that they are learning from recognized standards. It sends a powerful message that these emergency preparedness efforts are serious and credible. Certification becomes a badge of assurance, communicating that the skills learned are trusted and dependable when crises arise.

In enhancing the effectiveness of emergency preparedness training, involving local health professionals plays a crucial role. These professionals bring not only their expertise but also a sense of familiarity to the table. Their presence can make the training sessions more relatable and authoritative. Imagine having a local nurse or firefighter share real-life stories and experiences during training sessions. This personal touch can make the learning process more engaging and impactful. Participants are likely to feel more connected to the material, understanding that it's not just theoretical but grounded in practical reality. Furthermore, having familiar faces leading the training reinforces trust and encourages greater participation from the community.

Collaboration with local organizations can further bolster the training process. By partnering with these groups, churches can access additional resources while managing costs effectively. Local non-profits, health departments, or emergency management agencies might offer valuable tools, personnel, or financial aid to support training initiatives. Such partnerships can open doors to specialized equipment, educational materials, or even venues for conducting sessions. Additionally, working with established organizations enhances the visibility and legitimacy of the training program. Churches might find themselves part of a larger network of preparedness advocates, benefiting from shared knowledge and experience.

Fostering an open communication culture within the church is paramount for effective collaboration and response in emergencies. Open lines of communication ensure that all members feel included and informed, facilitating better teamwork and cooperation. Encouraging open dialogue provides a platform for sharing ideas, addressing concerns, and clarifying roles. For instance, holding regular meetings or forums where members can ask questions and voice opinions can significantly enhance the quality of the preparedness program. It allows for diverse perspectives to contribute to a more comprehensive plan, and everyone knows what to expect and how to contribute during an emergency.

To establish this open communication environment, church leaders should actively encourage feedback and suggestions. Setting up channels like suggestion boxes, surveys, or dedicated contact points can be beneficial. Imagine receiving input from congregants about preferred training times or areas they feel less confident in. This kind of information helps tailor the training to better meet the needs of the community. Moreover, by recognizing and implementing suggestions from members, leaders demonstrate that everyone's voice matters, fostering a sense of ownership and responsibility among the congregation.

Addressing unique needs is another important aspect of encouraging communication and collaboration. It's vital for church leaders to acknowledge that every member may have different requirements when it comes to emergency preparations. Some might need special assistance due to disabilities or other vulnerabilities, while others might require language or cultural considerations. Creating an inclusive preparedness plan involves understanding these unique needs and incorporating them into training sessions. Leaders could, for example, organize workshops that focus on specific challenges faced by different groups within the church, ensuring they receive appropriate support and attention.

Encouraging family involvement in emergency preparedness is another essential guideline. Families are foundational units of the church community, and their active participation can significantly enhance overall preparedness. When families work together to develop their emergency plans, it strengthens communal resilience and fosters a team-oriented mindset. Church leaders can facilitate this by organizing family-focused training days or providing materials that guide families in creating personalized emergency kits or evacuation plans. Engaging children through age-appropriate activities or discussions can also help instill awareness and readiness from a young age.

Another crucial aspect of preparedness planning is educating members thoroughly. Providing clear, concise guidelines on what to expect and how to act during emergencies empowers individuals to respond effectively. Education should cover basic procedures, potential risks, and available resources. Consider creating easy-to-understand checklists or visual aids that members can refer to when needed. Regularly updating and distributing such materials ensures that everyone remains informed and ready, reinforcing the importance of continuous learning and adaptation in the face of evolving threats.

Final Thoughts

In this chapter, we've explored how equipping church members with first aid and CPR skills is key to creating a well-prepared community. By bringing in certified trainers, churches ensure their congregations are learning the most current techniques in a hands-on way. Interactive sessions filled with role-playing make learning both practical and enjoyable, reinforcing what members need to know in real emergency situations. Regular refresher courses keep everyone's skills sharp, boosting confidence and readiness. Leaders have a big part to play, using these programs not just for individual safety but as a means of serving the wider community, while stories of personal impact can inspire others to join in.

We've also discussed the importance of regular evacuation drills and personal emergency plans. These elements help tailor and hone preparedness so everyone knows exactly what to do when it counts. Inclusivity ensures all members feel welcome, regardless of age or ability, making sure no one is left behind. Through open communication and community involvement, church leaders strengthen bonds and cultivate a collective spirit of preparedness that benefits everyone. With continuous practice and improvement, the church stands ready to face any challenge together.

Chapter 4

Creating a Culture of Readiness

Creating a culture of readiness in a church community is all about building the strength to face whatever comes our way. You know how everyone brings their unique talents and skills to make things happen? It's like that, but for when emergencies strike. Imagine your church as a woven fabric, where every member is a thread contributing to a stronger whole. This chapter dives into how you can enhance this resilience by fostering relationships within your church and with your neighbors. Whether it's through potlucks or game nights, these connections lay the groundwork for support when it matters most.

In this chapter, we'll explore practical ways to put this idea into action. We'll look at organizing neighborhood support networks, so you're not just relying on one another during services, but also prepared to lean on each other during crises. You'll see how emergency contact directories and collaboration with local organizations can make communication faster and responses more effective. The chapter outlines activities like workshops and drills designed to keep everyone engaged and informed. By the end, you'll have a better understanding of how to encourage readiness and resilience, ensuring your church community can stand strong together no matter what challenges arise.

Creating Neighborhood Support Networks

Creating a culture of readiness within a church community is much like weaving a tightly knit fabric. Each thread represents an individual, and together they form a strong tapestry that can withstand the trials and tribulations of emergencies. One of the foundational aspects of this culture is establishing and strengthening supportive networks both within the church and with neighboring communities to enhance collective safety.

The importance of forming local connections cannot be overstated. In times of need, a well-connected network can significantly quicken response times and provide necessary support. Imagine a situation where a sudden natural disaster strikes, and communication lines are down. Having pre-established relationships means there's already a plan in place, people you trust, and resources you can share without hesitation. It's like having an extended family ready to step in when one's own capabilities are stretched thin. Encouraging church members to know their neighbors and fostering relationships through simple initiatives like neighborhood picnics or regular check-ins can lay the groundwork for such connectivity. These efforts not only create bonds but also foster a sense of belonging and responsibility among community members.

Moreover, engaging all community members regularly is key to maintaining these bonds. Regular interactions don't have to be formal; they can be as simple as hosting a monthly potluck or organizing a game night. The benefits of these inclusive activities extend beyond mere socialization. They serve as platforms for interaction where people feel valued, heard, and included, thus breaking down any barriers of isolation or misunderstanding. Such gatherings can also double up as informal sessions where practical advice on emergency preparedness is exchanged naturally, reinforcing the notion that everyone has a role to play in ensuring collective safety.

Another practical tool in building a culture of readiness is the creation and use of emergency contact directories. Imagine having a comprehensive list of whom to call during varying emergencies – someone with medical expertise, another who knows first aid, and yet another with a generator or space for shelter. An emergency contact directory serves as a centralized resource for efficient communication. It's important to update it regularly and ensure it's accessible to all community members. Guidelines suggest periodically reviewing this list to include new members or remove outdated contacts. This continuity is crucial in maintaining the reliability and relevance of the directory.

Collaboration with neighboring churches and local organizations further broadens the safety net, expanding support systems beyond immediate church boundaries. Such alliances can bring about shared resources, pooled knowledge, and a more comprehensive approach to preparedness. For instance, partnering with the local fire department for basic firefighting training or joining hands with a nearby church to organize a community-wide awareness day can amplify the impact of readiness efforts. These collaborative partnerships not only bolster the capacity to respond effectively to emergencies but also build goodwill and camaraderie across different sectors of the community.

Developing Resilience-Building Activities

Creating a culture of readiness in the church community starts with initiating activities that not only educate congregants on disaster preparedness but also strengthen the bonds within the community. One effective way to achieve this is by hosting workshops focused on emergency preparedness, tailored specifically to address the risks relevant to your community. These workshops can cover a range of topics such as first-aid training, understanding local weather patterns, or plans for evacuation and sheltering-in-place. By tailoring these sessions to local concerns, you ensure that the information is not only relevant but immediately applicable to the participants' lives.

These workshops provide an excellent platform for members of the congregation to come together, share their experiences, and learn from one another. They serve as both an educational tool and a means of fostering stronger relationships among the parishioners. Encourage participation from various groups within the church, such as youth groups, senior citizens, and families, to ensure that preparedness becomes a shared responsibility across all ages and demographics. Inclusion ensures no member feels left out and encourages a sense of collective responsibility toward readiness.

Beyond theoretical knowledge, practical involvement is crucial. This is where engaging members in community service projects comes into play. These projects offer hands-on experience in skills critical to disaster response, like organizing emergency supplies, setting up communication chains, and providing support to vulnerable populations. Projects could include volunteering at local food banks, participating in clean-up drives, or assisting in neighborhood watch programs. Such activities build practical experience and instill a sense of ownership and responsibility within the community.

Organizing simulated emergency drills is another powerful method for enhancing preparedness. These simulations recreate potential emergency scenarios, allowing participants to practice their response strategies without the pressure of real danger. Drills should be designed to involve everyone—from children to older members—to better prepare them for actual emergencies. Consider collaborating with local emergency services to facilitate these exercises, as they can provide expert guidance and support. This collaboration not only improves the quality of the simulation but also strengthens ties with external organizations that are vital during any crisis.

A resilience resource library within the church can provide continuous learning opportunities long after workshops and drills have ended. This library can house books, pamphlets, online resources, and even video tutorials on various aspects of disaster readiness. Topics could range from psychological preparation to physical safety measures. Ensure that the resources are accessible to everyone; consider digital platforms for those who prefer online access, while maintaining physical copies for others. Encouraging congregants to contribute their own resources or review materials fosters a sense of shared learning and communal growth.

While planning these activities, it's essential to establish guidelines for organizing inclusive events that cater to the diverse needs of the church community. This includes considering accessibility for people with disabilities, creating childcare solutions during events, and accommodating different languages if necessary. Clear guidelines help ensure that every event is welcoming and productive, maximizing engagement and participation from the whole community.

Encouraging Volunteerism and Outreach

Creating a culture of readiness within church communities begins by fostering a strong volunteer ethos. The foundation lies in defining clear volunteer roles, allowing members to contribute effectively according to their unique skills and passions. Whether someone's talent is organizing, cooking, teaching, or manual labor, identifying these gifts and matching them with the right tasks not only enhances the efficiency of response efforts but also empowers individuals to serve joyfully.

Once roles are defined, it's essential to collaborate with local nonprofits and emergency services. By establishing these partnerships, churches gain access to valuable resources such as training, materials, and logistical support needed in times of crisis. Imagine volunteers participating in joint exercises with professionals, which not only sharpens their skills but also builds trust and a sense of camaraderie among all parties involved. This collaboration can be the key to unlocking resources otherwise inaccessible to the church alone, enhancing community resilience.

To further strengthen this culture of readiness, outreach initiatives can play a significant role. Hosting informational sessions and organizing community events allows church members to engage actively with preparedness topics. These gatherings may cover various scenarios, from natural disasters to unexpected societal challenges, equipping attendees with knowledge and strategies to face such situations. Setting up booths at community fairs or creating themed workshops can make learning about readiness less daunting and more engaging for everyone.

In advocating for a volunteer culture, the teachings of biblical service provide both inspiration and direction. Scripture offers numerous examples of selfless service, encouraging every member to embrace the spirit of helping others. Reminding the congregation that serving is an extension of faith encourages participation and commitment. Sharing stories from the Bible about individuals who stepped up during crises resonates deeply, motivating current generations to follow suit.

An important guideline here is organizing simulated emergencies or drills. Such activities put theory into practice, allowing volunteers to test their readiness in a controlled and safe environment. These simulations help identify potential gaps in coordination while providing learning opportunities to refine procedures. Regularly scheduled drills ensure that when a real emergency strikes, the response is swift, efficient, and confident.

Another vital component of nurturing a volunteer culture is hosting workshops on emergency preparedness. These educational sessions can be tailored to address community-specific risks, ensuring that participants leave with practical skills relevant to their environment. Workshops offer hands-on learning experiences, making it easier for attendees to grasp complex concepts and apply them confidently should the need arise.

Engaging in community service projects serves as yet another excellent initiative. These projects not only foster goodwill and enhance community bonds but also prepare volunteers for real-world emergency situations. Simple acts of service—whether cleaning up parks, helping the elderly, or organizing food drives—build a strong foundation of empathy and responsiveness within the church.

Additionally, creating a resilience resource library can become an invaluable tool for ongoing education. A well-stocked library with pamphlets, books, DVDs, and even online resources provides continuous learning opportunities for church members. This repository ensures that information is readily available and easily accessible, deepening the community's understanding of readiness over time.

By employing these strategies, church leaders actively cultivate an environment where volunteers feel valued, prepared, and inspired. Together, these efforts reinforce the church's role as a hub of support and strength, capable of responding to emergencies with grace and competence.

Implementing Practical Preparedness Measures

Creating a culture of readiness in church communities is an essential step toward ensuring resilience during emergencies. When church leaders focus on developing practical measures and resources, they empower their congregants to respond effectively in times of crisis. Let's explore how this can be achieved through specific strategies and teachings.

Start by developing emergency plans tailored to the local context. Every community has its own set of risks and threats, whether natural disasters, accidents, or public health emergencies. Begin by evaluating potential hazards unique to the area. For example, if your church is located in a flood-prone region, prioritize flood response and evacuation plans. Understanding these vulnerabilities helps create comprehensive emergency plans that address likely scenarios, making your preparation more relevant and effective.

Once you have a plan, promoting hands-on training sessions becomes crucial. These sessions equip church members with essential skills needed in emergencies, such as first aid, CPR, and basic firefighting techniques. Consider inviting professionals from local emergency services to conduct these workshops. Real-life practice is invaluable and empowers individuals to act confidently when every second counts. The hands-on approach not only builds competence but also fosters a sense of community as members learn and prepare together.

Continuously reviewing and updating preparedness measures ensures they stay relevant with evolving needs. Threats and best practices change over time, so routine assessments of your emergency plans are critical. Schedule regular meetings with your leadership team to evaluate the effectiveness of current strategies and make necessary adjustments. Additionally, encourage feedback from the congregation after drills or real incidents to identify areas for improvement. This dynamic process of review and refinement keeps your community agile and better prepared for any situation.

Stockpiling critical supplies is another important aspect of readiness. Assemble a collection of essential items like non-perishable food, water, medical supplies, flashlights, batteries, and blankets. Encourage each family within your church to maintain a similar stockpile at home, enhancing individual and communal resilience. Store these supplies in an accessible location within the church premises, clearly labeled for easy access during an emergency. Consider the specific needs of vulnerable groups, such as the elderly or those with mobility issues, when compiling your stock.

Utilizing digital tools for coordination can greatly enhance your preparedness efforts. Leverage technology to streamline communication and information sharing among church members. Create online platforms like group messaging apps or social media pages to distribute emergency alerts quickly. Digital calendars can help organize training sessions and distribution schedules for supplies. Moreover, digital maps with evacuation routes and safe zones provide an invaluable resource during an emergency.

Encouraging volunteerism plays a pivotal role in building a robust culture of readiness. Engage church members by defining clear roles and responsibilities related to emergency response. Some might serve on a first-aid team, while others could manage communications or logistics. Volunteers bring diverse skills and perspectives, enriching the community's collective preparedness. A spirit of service aligns with biblical teachings, fostering a deeper connection among congregants as they work toward a common goal.

Collaborating with local non-profits and emergency services can expand the church's resources and knowledge base. Establish partnerships with organizations specializing in disaster response or community health. These alliances provide valuable insights and additional support during crises. Joint exercises or collaborative events foster stronger relationships, ensuring smoother cooperation when most needed.

Lastly, creating outreach initiatives focused on education and awareness further strengthens preparedness culture. Host informational sessions or community events highlighting key aspects of emergency readiness. Invite guest speakers or use multimedia presentations to engage attendees effectively. These initiatives raise awareness and motivate broader participation, spreading crucial knowledge throughout the community.

Summary and Reflections

As we wrap up this chapter, let's take a moment to reflect on how building a culture of readiness can transform the resilience of a church community during tough times. We've explored the power of creating neighborhood support networks, where each member knows they have others to rely on when emergencies strike. By fostering strong local connections, members are equipped with quicker response times and shared resources, turning potential chaos into organized action. Whether it's through neighborhood events or emergency contact directories, these initiatives lay the groundwork for unity and preparedness.

We've also touched on practical ways to keep this momentum going—like engaging the community through workshops, volunteer efforts, and hands-on drills that make emergency preparedness a shared responsibility. The idea isn't just about being ready for what might happen but about building relationships and skills that strengthen the whole congregation. By collaborating with nearby organizations and harnessing technology for coordination, church leaders can ensure everyone is informed and involved. Each step brings congregants closer together, creating a robust support system that embodies the spirit of community care and collective strength.

Chapter 5

Integrating Faith with Preparedness

Integrating faith with preparedness is about blending spiritual values and practical readiness to create a resilient church community. When emergencies strike, having a plan that aligns with biblical teachings can make all the difference for both individuals and congregations as a whole. It's more than just knowing how to store supplies or set safety procedures in motion. It means embracing a mindset where faith and readiness walk hand-in-hand, helping each other flourish. By focusing on this balance, church leaders can nurture communities that are well-prepared to face challenges, guided by principles found within their faith.

In this chapter, we'll dive into how biblical stories provide valuable lessons in preparedness, offering examples of foresight and planning that have stood the test of time. We'll explore how personal spiritual strength can become an anchor during a crisis, providing resilience through verses like those found in Philippians. As we connect the power of scripture with practical steps, such as organizing supplies and communal efforts, we'll see how these age-old teachings can inspire collective action. Additionally, we'll look at the role of prayer in weaving together logistical plans with spiritual intentions, creating a preparedness strategy that's both meaningful and effective. By considering individual contributions within a community context, you'll discover how to empower your congregation to work together, ensuring no one faces challenges alone. Through holistic integration of faith and preparedness, this chapter aims to equip you with insights and strategies to lead your community toward greater resilience and unity.

Finding Scriptural Inspiration for Preparedness

In church communities, grounding emergency preparedness in scriptural teachings can be transformative. Take Joseph's story from the Book of Genesis as a starting point. When Pharaoh dreamed of seven years of plenty followed by seven years of famine, Joseph, through his faith and God-given wisdom, advised storing surplus grain during the abundant years. This foresight ensured Egypt's survival during scarcity. Church leaders might draw on this narrative to highlight the necessity of resource management and planning. Just as Joseph prepared for future challenges, churches too can learn to anticipate needs, making sure resources are available when the congregation faces hardship.

Transitioning from Joseph to more personal spiritual strength, Philippians 4:13 says, "I can do all things through Christ who strengthens me." This verse is particularly reassuring, reminding believers that their faith provides strength even amid uncertainty. In an emergency, it's easy to feel overwhelmed or helpless. However, trusting in divine support can embolden individuals and make them more resilient. Church leaders can encourage members to deepen their faith, believing that with spiritual conviction, they can face any crisis with courage and determination. This mindset not only empowers individuals but also inspires others around them.

Shifting the focus to community, Ecclesiastes 4:12 highlights the power of unity: "Though one may be overpowered, two can defend themselves. A cord of three strands is not quickly broken." This wisdom underscores the strength found in working together. In preparedness, communal efforts can lead to more effective outcomes compared to isolated efforts. Church communities have a unique advantage here; the shared bonds of fellowship naturally lend themselves to collaboration. Leaders should emphasize that everyone has a role to play, whether it's through organizing supplies, sharing knowledge, or offering emotional support. This collective approach helps ensure no one stands alone in times of need.

Incorporating prayer into planning serves a dual purpose. On one hand, it unites logistical efforts with spiritual intentions. On the other, it enriches the process, ensuring actions are not simply practical but also imbued with meaning. Imagine preparing an emergency plan and including moments of prayer throughout each phase. This practice could involve praying for guidance at the beginning, expressing gratitude for resources gathered, and seeking protection for the community. By weaving prayer into these efforts, preparations become more than just securing physical safety; they transform into spiritually enriching experiences that align with faith-based values.

Moreover, integrating prayer into such plans emphasizes that every effort made is a testament to one's trust in divine provision. This fusion of action and belief makes preparedness more holistic and ensures that while planning for physical safety, spiritual well-being is equally prioritized. During training sessions or drills, setting aside time for communal prayer can fortify faith and create a sense of shared purpose and resolve. It becomes a reminder that amidst strategies and resources, there's a higher strength that guides and sustains the community.

As church leaders strive to integrate these biblical principles into emergency preparedness, they cultivate a preparedness culture rooted in both practicality and spirituality. Joseph's narrative about resourcefulness, the strength espoused in Philippians, the unity conveyed by Ecclesiastes, and the spiritual synergy achieved through prayer—each of these elements contributes to building resilient, informed, and empowered church bodies ready to face emergencies.

Utilizing Faith-Based Mental Health Resources

When emergencies strike, they affect not only the physical safety of individuals but also their emotional and mental well-being. It's crucial for church leaders to explore how faith-based mental health support can be seamlessly integrated into their preparedness plans to address these emotional challenges effectively. One practical step is establishing partnerships with local faith-based mental health services. By forging these relationships ahead of time, churches can ensure that accessible resources are readily available when crises occur. This proactive approach allows congregations to tap into professional expertise that aligns with their faith values, providing holistic support that resonates deeply with their community members.

To truly empower congregations as hubs of support during emergencies, promoting mental health awareness and response training is essential. Training sessions can equip church members with the skills necessary to recognize signs of emotional distress and provide initial support to those in need. Understanding how stress and anxiety manifest, particularly in high-stress situations, helps ensure that each congregant can act as a first responder within their own community, offering empathy and basic guidance. This kind of empowerment fosters a sense of shared responsibility and resilience, enabling church communities to respond effectively during times of crisis.

Moreover, integrating prayer with mental health practices offers a dual benefit of spiritual solace and professional care for stress reduction. Prayer, an integral part of many religious practices, provides comfort and connection to a higher power, which can be profoundly soothing during stressful times. When combined with mental health strategies, such as mindfulness or breathing exercises, it creates a comprehensive approach that addresses both spiritual needs and psychological well-being. Encouraging this integration allows individuals to find peace and strength through their faith while benefiting from evidence-based mental health interventions.

After a crisis has passed, it's important to implement post-disaster support programs that focus on community-driven healing processes. These programs should aim to bring people together, fostering connections and reducing the stigma often associated with seeking mental health care. Church leaders can organize events or group discussions where members share experiences and feelings, creating a safe space for vulnerability and understanding. By normalizing conversations about mental health, church communities can help dismantle any lingering stigma, encouraging more individuals to seek the help they need and deserve.

Addressing mental health in the context of faith also means being open to learning and adapting. Just as physical readiness plans must evolve with new challenges and insights, so too should our approaches to mental health preparedness. Church leaders should remain committed to continuous education about mental health topics, ensuring they stay informed about best practices and emerging research. This commitment not only benefits their communities but also sets an example of growth and adaptability rooted in faith.

Furthermore, it's beneficial to create guidelines for incorporating prayer into overall preparedness efforts. By embedding spiritual practices in emergency drills and planning, church communities can ensure that their actions are anchored in faith, fostering a sense of calm and purpose even amidst chaos. For instance, beginning meetings or drills with a moment of prayer can remind participants of their shared beliefs and encourage unity. As congregations prepare for potential emergencies, this practice serves as a reminder of the spiritual dimensions of their actions, reinforcing the idea that faith and preparedness go hand in hand.

By implementing practical strategies for fostering cooperation and unity within their communities, church leaders can enhance both emotional and spiritual resilience. Facilitating regular gatherings or workshops focused on strengthening communal bonds ensures that individuals feel supported and valued. During these gatherings, it's helpful to emphasize the importance of collective effort and mutual support. Using analogies and stories from scripture that highlight themes of cooperation can motivate members to actively participate in preparedness initiatives, knowing that their contributions matter.

Aligning emergency planning with spiritual principles also plays a crucial role in establishing a strong foundation for both individuals and the larger congregation. Developing strategies that reflect core biblical teachings can guide decision-making and inspire action. By holding onto these spiritual principles, church leaders reinforce the notion that preparedness is not merely a logistical exercise but a manifestation of faith in action. It demonstrates a deep commitment to caring for one another, echoing the values taught within their religious communities.

Praying for Guidance and Protection

In times of crisis, prayer can serve as a beacon of hope and unity for church communities. When faced with uncertainty, gathering together in communal prayer creates a strong fabric of connection among members. This bond is not only spiritual but also offers emotional support, helping to ease the fears and anxieties that accompany unpredictability. As people pray together, they find solace and strength in shared resolve, reminding each other that they are not alone in their struggles. This unity fosters a sense of belonging and mutual support, which can be crucial during difficult times.

Having designated leaders for prayer initiatives can significantly enhance the spiritual readiness and morale of a congregation. By appointing individuals who are passionate about emergency preparedness and spiritually grounded, church communities can ensure that their approach to crises remains faith-driven. These leaders can organize regular prayer meetings that focus on specific aspects of emergency preparedness, such as praying for wisdom in decision-making or safety during an emergency. A structured approach to prayer initiatives provides consistency and ensures that the community remains spiritually engaged and prepared, regardless of the challenges they face.

Furthermore, integrating prayer into emergency drills and planning activities allows church communities to anchor their preparedness efforts in faith. By starting an emergency drill with a prayer, members are reminded that their actions should reflect their beliefs and values. This integration ensures that preparedness practices are not just mechanical routines but are also spiritually meaningful endeavors. It encourages participants to consider how their faith informs their behavior in emergencies, fostering resilience that combines both spiritual and physical readiness.

An effective way to illustrate the transformative role of prayer during crises is by collecting testimonials from those who have experienced its benefits. Hearing stories from individuals who have felt uplifted and supported by prayer during challenging times can be incredibly inspiring. These testimonials not only provide concrete examples of prayer's impact but also reinforce the belief that faith can play a powerful role in preparedness efforts. Sharing these stories within the church community can motivate others to embrace prayer as a key component of their preparedness strategy, ensuring that future responses to crises are guided by faith.

When establishing structured approaches, it is beneficial to assign designated leaders to take charge of prayer initiatives. This leadership structure helps maintain focus and direction, ensuring that prayer remains a central element in emergency preparedness. Leaders can coordinate efforts, plan relevant activities, and encourage participation, making sure that prayer initiatives are aligned with the church's broader goals. By having this structure in place, church communities can effectively sustain spiritual readiness and morale over time, creating a cohesive and resilient response to any crisis.

Encouraging Community Engagement and Responsibility

In church communities, the responsibility of each individual is a powerful theme that can be effectively communicated through scripture. One passage that beautifully illustrates this idea is 1 Corinthians 12:12-14, which compares the community to a body and emphasizes that every member has a role that is crucial to the whole. This concept not only enhances the spiritual unity within the congregation but also fosters a sense of duty when it comes to preparedness efforts. When members of the church understand that each person's contribution is significant, they are more likely to participate actively in emergency readiness initiatives.

For church leaders, drawing connections between biblical stories and current needs for preparedness can be an enlightening approach. This means looking at familiar narratives and identifying lessons that can apply to modern-day challenges. For example, just as ancient figures made preparations for their communities, today, there are practical steps we must take to ensure everyone's safety. Leaders who highlight these parallels can inspire action that addresses both spiritual guidance and tangible preparedness measures, motivating congregations to think beyond the spiritual aspects.

Another practical step is organizing faith-based preparedness workshops. These workshops provide an excellent opportunity for combining technical skills with community-building activities. By offering training sessions on topics such as first aid, food storage, or communication plans during emergencies, congregations not only gain valuable knowledge but also strengthen their sense of community. The interactive nature of these workshops enhances relationships and commitments among the members, as they learn together and support one another. Such events help solidify collective responsibility towards each other's well-being.

To maintain high levels of engagement, regular scriptural reflections can be integrated into these preparedness efforts. By weaving in biblical teachings relevant to preparedness, church leaders can keep the topic alive in the minds of their congregants. Incorporating testimonials from those who have been touched by past experiences or witnessed the power of being prepared can further emphasize the importance of ongoing efforts. These personal stories serve as reminders of how faith and preparedness intersect meaningfully in real-life situations.

Encouraging open communication and collaborative action within the church community is essential. When members feel like they are part of a larger mission guided by shared beliefs, they are more motivated to contribute. Through open dialogue and inclusive planning processes, members can voice concerns, share ideas, and offer solutions to potential challenges in emergency management. This sense of belonging and collective problem-solving strengthens the community's ability to respond cohesively during crises.

Summary and Reflections

This chapter has taken a deep dive into weaving biblical principles with practical emergency preparedness, offering church leaders a rounded approach to boosting resilience within their communities. Through stories of resourcefulness, like Joseph's grain storage in Genesis, we see the value of strategic planning and foresight. Such narratives guide us in making sure resources are available during tough times. By drawing strength from scriptures like Philippians 4:13, members are empowered to rely on faith when facing unpredictability. And Ecclesiastes 4:12 reminds us that unity is our greatest asset—when individuals come together, they form an unbreakable bond. Integrating prayer into these preparations not only aligns efforts with spiritual beliefs but also ensures each step is meaningful.

With this understanding, church communities can build a culture of preparedness rooted in both spirituality and practicality. Encouraging participation in emergency plans by highlighting each member's role fosters a strong sense of collaboration. This collective effort strengthens bonds and emphasizes everyone's contribution. By combining faith-based guidance with practical steps, church leaders create a holistic strategy that addresses physical safety while nurturing mental and spiritual well-being. Through regular practice and prayerful involvement, congregations stand ready to face any challenges together, grounded in their shared faith and purpose.

Chapter 6

Collaborating with Local Authorities

Collaborating with local authorities opens up a world of opportunities for churches to bolster their community safety and preparedness plans. Churches are more than just places of worship; they're cornerstones of their communities. By working hand-in-hand with local fire departments, police, and other emergency services, church leaders can transform these institutions into lifelines during unexpected crises. Imagine having systems in place that not only keep your congregation safe but also extend a helping hand to neighbors in need. Through purposeful collaboration, churches can lead the way in creating safer environments for everyone.

In this chapter, we'll delve into how strengthening partnerships with local authorities can enhance crisis response efforts. We start by exploring practical ways for churches to establish formal partnerships, ensuring both sides understand their roles and responsibilities during emergencies. We'll also discuss the importance of clear communication channels, like regular meetings and memorandums of understanding, to keep everyone on the same page. You'll learn about participating in community-wide drills to gain firsthand experience alongside emergency responders and improve preparedness plans based on real-time feedback. Additionally, we will cover how churches can leverage training programs offered by local agencies to equip their members with essential skills. By the end of the chapter, you'll have a clearer picture of the many ways these collaborations reinforce community ties and readiness, ultimately fostering a resilient, united front against any crisis.

Establishing Formal Partnerships

When developing effective alliances between churches and local authorities for emergency response, the first step is understanding and tapping into the wealth of expertise that fire, police, and emergency management departments provide. Churches can start by initiating open dialogues with these agencies to identify shared goals and concerns related to community safety. These discussions can evolve into strategic collaborations where both parties agree on how they can best support one another during a crisis. For instance, church leaders might coordinate with local fire departments to understand evacuation protocols and fire safety measures, ensuring the community is prepared and informed. Similarly, engaging with police departments can enhance security measures within church premises while ensuring a swift response in case of emergencies. By establishing these connections, churches not only gain access to expert advice but also establish themselves as proactive partners in maintaining public safety.

Drafting Memorandums of Understanding (MOUs) is another crucial aspect of forming alliances with local authorities. An MOU serves as a formal document outlining each party's roles and responsibilities during crises, preventing potential misunderstandings when time is of the essence. This document can specify what resources the church will make available, such as space for emergency shelters or volunteers to assist in relief efforts, in exchange for the expertise and resources offered by emergency services. These agreements instill a sense of accountability and readiness, ensuring that both the church and local authorities are aligned in their emergency response strategies. It's important to revisit and update MOUs periodically to reflect any new developments or changes in circumstances, reinforcing the commitment to a collaborative partnership.

Regular meetings between church representatives and local authorities are vital for assessing the effectiveness of existing arrangements and making necessary adjustments. Such gatherings provide a platform to discuss recent experiences, analyze what worked well, and identify areas for improvement. They also allow for sharing updates about new resources, contact persons, or procedural changes within local agencies. By maintaining ongoing communication, churches can stay informed about potential threats or emergency scenarios relevant to their community. These meetings can be informal yet structured enough to ensure all important topics are covered. Moreover, fostering interpersonal relationships through consistent interaction enhances trust and cooperation, which are critical during stressful situations.

Participation in training programs offered by local agencies is an excellent way for church communities to develop essential crisis-response skills. These programs often include workshops and simulation exercises that equip participants with practical knowledge and improve their ability to respond effectively in emergencies. Whether it's learning basic first aid, understanding search and rescue operations, or becoming adept at crowd management during evacuations, these skills empower church members to act promptly and confidently during crises. Additionally, such trainings create opportunities for building rapport with responders and other community stakeholders, reinforcing the network of support needed during critical times.

Participating in Community-Wide Drills

Gaining practical experience and enhancing collaboration through community drills is an essential aspect of strengthening partnerships with local authorities. By working closely with emergency response teams, church leaders can observe and learn valuable lessons that can significantly improve their emergency plans. Witnessing how these experts operate during a drill provides insights into the necessary procedures and equipment required for effective crisis management. This learning process allows churches to tailor their emergency plans specifically, ensuring they are not only comprehensive but also aligned with best practices in the field.

One of the most important outcomes of participating in community drills is building trust and cooperation with emergency responders. When church leaders and congregations engage in simulated scenarios alongside first responders, it creates an opportunity for both parties to become familiar with each other's roles and expectations. This collaborative environment fosters mutual respect and understanding, which is crucial during actual emergencies. Knowing that local authorities are familiar faces who have practiced alongside them, church communities can feel more confident and prepared when real situations arise.

Drills are not just about practicing responses; they are also invaluable opportunities to refine existing disaster response plans based on real-time feedback. After conducting a drill, taking time to debrief and discuss what worked well and where improvements can be made is key. This iterative process ensures that each exercise results in a stronger, more efficient plan. It involves evaluating communication methods, decision-making processes, and resource allocation strategies. The feedback gleaned from these exercises enables church leaders to make informed adjustments to protocols, thereby enhancing the overall preparedness of the congregation. Effective communication is critical in this context. Regular dialogue between church representatives and local authorities is essential to ensure alignment in disaster response protocols. Setting up ongoing meetings helps maintain a clear flow of information and allows both sides to address any concerns or changes promptly.

Participating in community drills is also an excellent way to strengthen ties with other local organizations and residents, fostering a resilient community. These exercises often involve various community stakeholders, including schools, businesses, and non-profits, creating a network of support and shared resources. Through joint participation, churches can establish partnerships that extend beyond drills and into everyday interactions, promoting goodwill and cooperation. Engaging with other groups in the community contributes to a collective readiness that benefits everyone involved. In times of crisis, having pre-established relationships with diverse community members ensures a coordinated and unified approach to managing disasters. Furthermore, involving the wider community in drills brings about an awareness of the church's role as a support hub, encouraging more people to seek assistance or contribute help when needed.

While participating in training programs with emergency response teams is one avenue to enhance preparedness, regular communication and aligning disaster response protocols are equally vital. Churches should be proactive in reaching out to local authorities to discuss potential risks and develop strategies collaboratively. Establishing lines of communication before an emergency strikes lays the groundwork for quick and effective responses when time is of the essence. Guidelines for these communications can include setting up routine check-ins and updating contact lists regularly to ensure swift access to critical information.

Ultimately, the goal of engaging in community drills and building these relationships is to create a safe and supportive environment for all members of the church and the broader community. By observing and learning from emergency response teams, churches not only gain valuable knowledge but also demonstrate their commitment to safeguarding their congregations. This proactive stance encourages a culture of preparedness that permeates throughout the church community, making everyone more vigilant and capable in the face of adversity.

Sharing Resources and Information

In times of emergency, a church's role as a central hub is vital. By centralizing critical emergency information within the church, leaders can streamline updates and protocols efficiently. Think of it as having all your important documents neatly organized in one place instead of scattered everywhere. This way, when a crisis hits, no time is lost scrambling for what's needed. Clear communication channels should be established, like designated team members responsible for specific tasks, so everyone knows their role and remains informed about any changes.

Imagine a network where churches, local businesses, and other community organizations work together, exchanging resources such as volunteers, supplies, and facilities. Establishing these networks before an emergency ensures smoother cooperation when it's truly needed. For instance, if one church has extra space but lacks certain supplies, they could connect with another organization to balance out those needs. By fostering such relationships, communities become more resilient, as there's always a backup plan or a helping hand available in times of need.

Co-hosting information sessions with local authorities can play a significant part in educating both church members and the wider community about emergency procedures. Let's face it: the more people know what to do during a crisis, the better prepared everyone will be. These sessions can cover various topics, from basic first aid to understanding evacuation routes. Not only does this empower individuals, but it also strengthens the bond between the church and local authorities, showing a united front to the community.

A guideline here would be beneficial. When organizing these sessions, consider inviting local emergency response teams to lead specific talks or demonstrations. Their expertise provides attendees with real-world insights. Moreover, encouraging interactive Q&A sessions can address particular concerns or misunderstandings, ensuring that everyone leaves the session feeling more informed and secure about what steps to take and how to react in an emergency.

Updating emergency plans regularly based on shared experiences is equally important. No one wants to be caught off guard because they're relying on outdated procedures. After each incident or drill, take some time to assess what worked well and what didn't. Gathering feedback from everyone involved — from the leadership team to the volunteers — offers diverse perspectives and insights, allowing you to refine the emergency plan continuously.

For example, perhaps a previous drill revealed confusion around communication methods. In that case, future plans might include additional training or alternative ways to convey critical information swiftly. This continuous cycle of learning and adaptation ensures that the church's emergency plans stay relevant and effective.

Participating in community-wide drills offers invaluable experience and helps in refining plans further. These drills simulate actual emergencies, providing a safe environment to test preparedness without real-world consequences. Being part of such exercises allows churches to observe emergency responders in action, teaching them how best to tailor their internal procedures. Additionally, drills build trust and cooperation, reinforcing ties not just with local authorities but also other community organizations and residents.

Understanding community dynamics plays a crucial role as well. Each community is unique, with its own set of challenges and resources. By being aware of these nuances, churches can tailor their preparedness efforts accordingly. For instance, suppose a particular area tends to flood during heavy rains. In that case, the church might prioritize stockpiling sandbags or identifying safe locations for temporary shelter. Acknowledging and respecting these local intricacies fosters greater collaboration and harmony within the community.

Utilizing drills not solely for testing but also for refining plans based on real-time feedback helps improve overall effectiveness. Maybe during a drill, it becomes evident that a specific communication line is unreliable. In such instances, it's essential to explore alternatives, ensuring every aspect of the emergency plan operates smoothly. This iterative process bolsters confidence among all stakeholders, proving that the church is well-prepared for whatever comes its way.

Creating Memorandums of Understanding (MOUs) with local authorities enhances collaboration by clearly defining roles and expectations during crises. An MOU acts as a formal agreement, laying the groundwork for mutual support and cooperation. By developing these agreements, churches ensure everyone knows exactly what to do when an emergency arises, reducing any potential confusion or overlap. Moreover, MOUs often lead to more frequent interactions and discussions, paving the way for ongoing improvements and strengthened partnerships.

Building Community Connections

Strengthening the bonds between church communities and local authorities can significantly enhance preparedness during crises. One effective way to foster these relationships is by hosting or joining local events such as clean-ups and educational workshops. These activities not only encourage active participation but also build a sense of teamwork and trust among community members. Imagine organizing a neighborhood clean-up day where church volunteers and local residents work side by side, picking up litter and planting flowers. Such an event serves as a platform for individuals to connect with one another while working towards a common goal. Educational workshops on emergency preparedness offer opportunities to learn from local experts and share valuable information.

Supporting each other during disasters is crucial. Churches can play a vital role by pooling shared resources and offering shelter and essentials to those in need. Picture this: a major storm hits your town, leaving many families without power or safe living conditions. The church opens its doors as a temporary refuge, providing warm meals, blankets, and a place to stay until it is safe to return home. By coordinating with local authorities, church communities can create comprehensive support systems that include access to medical care and transportation to ensure safety and well-being. This collaborative effort strengthens community ties and demonstrates the commitment of churches to serve beyond their congregations.

Encouraging participation in preparedness activities not only equips people with vital skills but also promotes mutual aid and collective responsibility. One way to achieve this is by organizing regular drills and simulations that involve both church members and local authorities. These exercises help everyone understand their roles during emergencies, ensuring smooth coordination when real incidents occur. Additionally, by inviting local emergency responders to lead these activities, church leaders can boost confidence and cultivate a culture of readiness within their communities. Participation in preparedness activities instills a sense of ownership and accountability, encouraging individuals to take responsibility for their safety and the safety of others.

Accessing training and resources provided by local authorities is essential for elevating church preparedness levels. Many local government agencies offer free or low-cost training programs designed to improve emergency response skills. By participating in these programs, church leaders and congregation members gain practical knowledge that can be applied during crises. There are valuable resources available, including guidelines on creating emergency plans, tips for effective communication, and recommendations for stockpiling necessary supplies. Furthermore, attending workshops hosted by local authorities allows for interaction with professionals who can provide insights into specific challenges faced by church communities.

Creating resource exchange networks is a fantastic way for churches to collaborate with local authorities and other community organizations. By establishing these networks, churches can share supplies, manpower, and expertise efficiently. For instance, during an unforeseen event like a pandemic, resource exchange networks enable churches to distribute food, hygiene products, and masks swiftly to those most in need. To set up such a network, consider forming a committee comprised of representatives from various stakeholder groups to oversee exchanges and logistics. Regular meetings and open communication will ensure the network runs smoothly, fostering a spirit of cooperation and mutual support within the community.

Co-hosting information sessions with local authorities is another effective strategy to enhance community ties through collaborative preparedness efforts. These sessions provide a platform for sharing valuable knowledge and educating the community on procedures to follow during emergencies. By partnering with fire departments, police, and other emergency services, churches can offer attendees first-hand insights from experts. These sessions may cover topics such as evacuation routes, severe weather precautions, and basic first aid techniques. Everyone leaves better informed about actions they can take to protect themselves and their loved ones.

Engaging in regular meetings with local officials is key to maintaining strong partnerships and addressing any concerns promptly. Scheduling routine check-ins with representatives from local authorities ensures open lines of communication and enables swift action when needed. These meetings provide an opportunity to discuss developments in community safety initiatives, evaluate collaboration effectiveness, and explore new avenues for partnership. Having established relationships with local authorities before a crisis occurs means that churches are more likely to receive timely assistance, further bolstering community resilience.

Final Thoughts

As we wrap up our discussion on strengthening partnerships, it's clear that joining hands with local authorities can make a huge difference when it comes to community safety during emergencies. By building formal relationships and engaging in open communication, churches can tap into the expertise of fire, police, and emergency services. Drafting MOUs helps clarify roles and responsibilities, ensuring everyone is on the same page when crises arise. Regular meetings and participation in training programs bolster preparedness and foster trust—a crucial component when stress levels peak.

Being part of community drills and sharing resources further enhances collaboration and readiness. These activities aren't just practice—they're opportunities to refine plans, establish comradeship, and invite wider community engagement. Imagine knowing exactly whom to turn to when disaster strikes—whether it's sharing facilities or information, you've already built those bridges. By working together, church leaders and local authorities set up a resilient support system ready to face challenges head-on. The real takeaway here? Stronger partnerships lead to safer communities, empowering everyone involved to handle emergencies effectively and confidently.

Chapter 7

Ensuring Effective Communication During Crises

Effective communication during crises is essential for maintaining a strong connection within church communities. In times of uncertainty, ensuring that everyone stays informed and engaged can help ease anxiety and build resilience. Today's digital age offers numerous tools to facilitate this connection, allowing church leaders to communicate swiftly with their congregation. From social media platforms to email newsletters, utilizing diverse channels means messages can reach people wherever they are most comfortable engaging. It's not just about sending out information but fostering ongoing conversations where the community feels heard and cared for.

This chapter dives into the practicalities of using multiple communication methods to keep congregations connected during challenging times. We'll explore how social media can be used for instant updates and engagement, while email newsletters serve as a channel for more detailed information. Additionally, the role of text messaging will be examined for its ability to deliver urgent alerts quickly. We won't forget those who prefer traditional methods; community bulletin boards still have their place in reaching non-tech-savvy members. By understanding these various approaches, church leaders can craft a tailored communication strategy that caters to the diverse needs of their congregation, ensuring no one is left out of the loop in times of crisis.

Implementing Multiple Communication Channels

In a world where digital connectivity plays an increasingly pivotal role, utilizing diverse communication methods can ensure that every member of your congregation stays informed and engaged during crises. Social media platforms have become a key tool for reaching out to large

FAITHFUL PREPPING SECURITY IN SPIRIT 53

numbers of people effectively. By leveraging platforms such as Facebook, Twitter, or Instagram, church leaders can share real-time updates, insights, and even words of encouragement. These tools allow for instant interaction, which can be a blessing in times of uncertainty, catering to a broad audience with varied age groups. It's important to remember that social media is not just about broadcasting messages but also about listening. Engaging with congregants' comments and questions fosters a sense of community and helps address concerns swiftly.

However, while social media is excellent for quick updates, it's often not the best medium for detailed information. This is where email newsletters come into play. Email remains one of the most direct ways to communicate detailed plans and consistent updates. It ensures that all relevant information is conveyed thoroughly, allowing members to stay prepared and reducing confusion. A well-structured newsletter can include everything from the schedule of events, safety protocols, to messages from the leadership team. Additionally, emails can be archived easily, enabling recipients to reference past communications when needed. Churches might consider varying their email content with multimedia elements like videos or infographics to keep it engaging.

Another powerful tool in crisis communication is text messaging. When there's a need for urgent and immediate communication, text messages are invaluable. They offer wide accessibility across age demographics, ensuring that important alerts reach members quickly. Whether it's a weather-related cancellation or a last-minute change in venue, a simple text message can make all the difference. Many services now offer mass texting capabilities, allowing leaders to send a single message that reaches everyone on their list. Texting also allows for brief exchanges of information or inquiries, should a congregant need immediate clarification.

Not everyone is entrenched in digital modes of communication—this is where more traditional methods still hold significant value. Community bulletin boards, placed in strategic locations around the church premises, can serve non-tech-savvy members by providing tangible access to critical information. Bulletins can display vital information like emergency contact numbers, schedules, and meeting points during crises. The physical presence of these boards can also act as a comforting reminder of stability and continuity within the church community.

Implementing multiple communication channels effectively requires some thoughtful planning and action. Starting with crafting a dedicated communication strategy that incorporates various mediums can ensure messages reach their intended audiences. Church leaders should assess which platforms are most used by their congregants and tailor strategies accordingly. Training a dedicated communication team is essential to manage these diverse channels efficiently. These individuals can monitor the platforms, respond to queries, and adapt messages as situations develop.

Furthermore, incorporating feedback mechanisms is crucial. After implementing this multi-channel approach, it's beneficial to gather insights from the congregation about what works best. Surveys or suggestion boxes can provide valuable feedback, helping refine and optimize future communications. Being open to suggestions and ready to adapt shows congregants that the leadership values their input, fostering trust and cooperation.

While consistency and clarity are always important, during crises, they become vital. Each communication method should reinforce a unified message, avoiding any misinformation or conflicting reports. Providing regular updates, even if there is no new information to convey, can reassure your congregation, letting them know they are not forgotten amidst the turmoil.

Designating Spokespersons and Liaisons

One of the crucial elements in ensuring effective communication during crises within a church community is establishing a chain of communication with designated leaders. This approach begins with appointing primary and backup spokespersons, creating a clear path for information dissemination. Having identifiable figures responsible for communicating vital information not only ensures clarity but also fosters trust among congregants. People look to these leaders for guidance during uncertain times, making their role pivotal in maintaining calm and order.

In such challenging circumstances, it's essential that these spokespersons are well-trained in public speaking and crisis management. Training helps them articulate messages that align with the church's values while enhancing their authority. By speaking coherently and confidently, they can mitigate panic and misinformation. For instance, real-life scenarios and role-playing exercises can prepare them to handle media inquiries or address large groups effectively. Such preparation ensures that messages conveyed are consistent and reassuring, grounding the congregation in truth and stability.

Building relationships with local emergency services is another fundamental aspect of crisis communication. Collaboration with police, fire departments, and medical teams allows churches to share resources and expertise. These partnerships can provide valuable updates and aid in coordinating responses during emergencies. Imagine a situation where an emergency service knows the layout and key contact points within your church; this familiarity could save precious time and lives. Moreover, being in close communication with these external bodies enhances the credibility of the information being shared by church leaders, as congregants know these updates are backed by professionals.

Furthermore, involving the community in the communication strategy greatly contributes to effective crisis management. By encouraging congregation members to take on roles, whether it's as part of a communication team or a feedback committee, you foster a sense of ownership and engagement. Individuals involved in these roles can serve as liaisons between the leadership and the broader community, promoting two-way communication. Gathering feedback from congregants post-crisis can reveal insights and areas for improvement, ensuring that future communications are even more responsive and tailored to the community's needs.

Maintaining a robust internal communication system is also critical. Churches should have reliable methods in place to reach all members swiftly. This includes utilizing phone trees, email lists, and dedicated apps or platforms where messages can be relayed quickly. Ensuring that there's a back-up plan, like manual call chains or physical bulletin boards, guarantees that communication lines remain open, even if one method fails. A well-organized system reflects a church's preparedness and commitment to keeping everyone informed, safe, and united.

Designating spokespersons and building a communication chain are not just operational tasks; they're about empowering individuals who can stand as pillars of support when it matters most. Clear guidelines on who communicates what, when, and through which channels streamline efforts and minimize confusion. It's worth recognizing that every member of the church community has a role to play, whether in sharing accurate information or providing support to one another. This collective effort transforms the church from just a place of worship to a beacon of hope and resilience during trying times.

Additionally, offering continuous education and aligning these practices with church teachings reinforces the trust placed in leadership. It's about embodying the very principles that are preached, demonstrating care and responsibility in action. As churches navigate the complexities of crises, understanding each other's strengths and limitations fosters a culture of unity and mutual respect. The collaboration between spiritual values and practical measures creates a holistic approach to crisis management.

Developing Contingency Communication Plans

In times of crisis, having a well-structured communication strategy is crucial for any organization, including churches. These strategies not only ensure that accurate information is shared swiftly but also promote a sense of safety and community among congregants. Developing contingency communication plans for different crisis scenarios helps church leaders provide timely, specific guidance. The key here is to have tailored plans for various crises, whether it's a natural disaster, health emergency, or security threat. Each plan should include clear instructions on roles and responsibilities, ensuring everyone knows what to do. By crafting these targeted plans, churches can respond quickly and effectively, minimizing confusion and enhancing safety for everyone involved.

Conducting regular drills is another essential aspect of effective crisis communication. Drills offer an opportunity to practice the communication plan in real time, allowing church members to understand their roles and become familiar with procedures. Through these rehearsals, potential weaknesses in the plan can be identified and rectified. For instance, a drill might reveal that certain messages are unclear or that more training is needed for specific individuals. Regular drills not only reinforce knowledge but also help instill confidence among the congregation, knowing that the church is prepared to handle emergencies efficiently. It's important to treat these drills as learning experiences, where feedback is welcomed and improvements are continuously made.

Evaluating communication technologies is fundamental to ensuring that all members receive important updates, especially during a crisis. With a variety of channels available—from emails and text alerts to social media posts—it's crucial to prioritize methods that best reach your entire audience. Some technologies might be more suited to immediate alerts, while others provide detailed information or facilitate ongoing discussions. When evaluating these tools, consider factors such as accessibility, user-friendliness, and reliability. For example, while older members may prefer phone calls or text messages, younger congregants might engage more with digital platforms like apps or social media. Understanding these preferences allows the church to leverage technology effectively, making sure no one is left out of the loop during critical moments.

Feedback mechanisms following drills and actual emergencies play a vital role in refining communication strategies. After each event, gathering insights from participants and reviewing what went well and what could be improved offers invaluable data for future planning. Encouraging open dialogue about the experience not only helps adapt strategies to better fit the community's needs but also fosters a culture of transparency and continuous improvement. This feedback loop enables church leaders to make informed decisions and adaptations, ensuring that their communication remains effective and relevant. Whether it's adjusting the frequency of updates or changing the platform used, these refinements contribute to a more resilient communication strategy that can withstand various challenges.

Ensuring Accessibility and Inclusivity in Communication

In times of crisis, effective communication is essential, but it must also be inclusive. Church leaders have a responsibility to ensure that everyone in their congregation receives important messages without barriers. Making communication methods accessible is not merely a technical endeavor; it's an embodiment of the church's commitment to inclusivity.

One key approach is incorporating alt-text and employing plain language. Alt-text serves as a description for images on digital platforms, crucial for those with visual impairments who rely on screen readers. Imagine your church shares a graphic with vital information about a community shelter during a crisis. Without alt-text, this information could be lost to a blind member. Adding detailed descriptions bridges this gap, ensuring comprehension across abilities. Similarly, using plain language eliminates jargon and complexity, making messages clear to individuals with cognitive disabilities or lower literacy skills. A good rule of thumb is to keep sentences short and direct, and avoid unnecessary technical terms. This way, everyone can understand the message at first glance, helping to reduce anxiety and confusion in stressful situations.

For video communications, providing accessibility features like sign language interpretations or subtitles can significantly extend inclusivity. Videos are a powerful medium for conveying emotions and detailed instructions during emergencies. However, without these accommodations, those who are deaf or hard of hearing might miss out on critical updates. By integrating real-time sign language interpreters during live broadcasts or adding subtitles to pre-recorded videos, you ensure that no one feels isolated from the communal experience of receiving guidance and support. It's worth noting that many platforms offer tools to automate subtitle creation, which can save time while reaching broader audiences.

Accessibility efforts in communication reflect a deeper commitment of the church to inclusivity. When congregants see that their needs are considered, it fosters a sense of belonging and reassurance that the church truly cares for each individual. It shows respect for diversity and acknowledges the uniqueness of every individual within the community. For example, a member with a disability may feel more valued and appreciated when they witness their church actively taking steps to accommodate their needs. Furthermore, such actions often inspire similar inclusive behaviors in other areas of church life, promoting an atmosphere where everyone is encouraged to participate fully, regardless of their physical or cognitive abilities.

Regularly testing and adapting communication tools is another crucial aspect of maintaining inclusivity. Technology is always evolving, and what works today might become obsolete tomorrow. Therefore, conducting periodic reviews of the church's communication strategies helps identify potential gaps and areas for improvement. This practice might involve gathering feedback from the congregation about the accessibility of recent communications, or testing new software that could better serve those with disabilities. Encouraging open dialogue and suggestions ensures that the church remains responsive to the needs of its members. Moreover, it allows leaders to stay informed about emerging technologies that could enhance communication effectiveness.

Adapting communication methods based on the nature of the crisis can guide churches to make thoughtful decisions. Some situations may require rapid dissemination of information, while others need more detailed explanations. Therefore, having flexible plans tailored to various scenarios ensures that messages remain clear and purposeful, ultimately aiding in keeping everyone informed and safe. For instance, during a natural disaster, quick alerts through text messages might be crucial, whereas a public health advisory might benefit from comprehensive emails with links to additional resources.

Ensuring accessibility is not just about compliance; it's about embodying the values of community care and respect. As church leaders strive to provide equal access to information, they pave the way toward a more inclusive and united congregation. In doing so, they reinforce the idea that everyone, regardless of their abilities, plays a vital role in the strength of the community.

Summary and Reflections

Navigating a crisis can feel overwhelming, but having a solid communication plan in place makes all the difference. This chapter highlighted how using multiple channels—like social media, emails, texts, and even traditional bulletin boards—can help church leaders keep everyone informed and connected. It's all about finding the right mix to reach different folks where they are most comfortable. Each method has its strengths, whether it's speedy updates or detailed newsletters, and integrating them ensures every member feels involved and up-to-date.

One key takeaway is the importance of designating spokespersons and nurturing partnerships with local emergency services. This ensures that when things get hectic, there's a clear voice offering guidance and information. By training these individuals in public speaking and crisis management, churches can provide reassuring communication that aligns with their values. Just remember, while the technology and strategies might seem complex at first, they're ultimately about making sure your community feels safe, heard, and valued during challenging times. So, as you build and refine these plans, think of them as essential tools that not only manage crises but also strengthen the bonds within your congregation.

Chapter 8

Building a Legacy of Safety and Preparedness

Building a legacy of safety and preparedness in a church community involves much more than preparing for the unexpected—it's about creating a lasting foundation that future leaders can rely on. This chapter dives into the importance of establishing a culture where safety isn't an afterthought but is embedded into each aspect of church life. Imagine a place where everyone, from seasoned church members to energetic newcomers, understands their role in keeping the community secure, drawing from past experiences to improve current practices.

Through this chapter, we explore various methods to instill such a culture. We'll see how important it is to document lessons learned from earlier incidents, ensuring knowledge isn't lost over time. You'll discover how creating a centralized repository of reports can serve as a vital tool for handling emergencies as they arise. Additionally, fostering open dialogue and holding debriefings after events are discussed as ways to ensure continuous learning and improvement. As you read, you'll also learn about engaging the entire community in these efforts and why involving everyone is beneficial. By diving into these strategies, you'll gain insight into building not just a prepared congregation but one united by a shared commitment to resilience and safety.

Documenting Lessons Learned from Past Incidents

Creating a legacy of safety and preparedness within a church community is about more than just preparing for the next emergency—it's about equipping future leaders with the tools they need to handle whatever comes their way. One powerful approach is to establish a comprehensive knowledge base, which serves as both a resource and a guide for those who will lead after us. Such a resource helps ensure that lessons learned from past experiences are not forgotten and that new leaders can build on the strong foundations laid by their predecessors.

A centralized repository of detailed reports on past emergencies is crucial in this endeavor. Think of it as a living library, filled with real-world wisdom accumulated over time. This repository should include accounts of what happened, how people responded, the effectiveness of those responses, and recommendations for future actions. By referring to these detailed reports, future leaders can gain valuable insights into past incidents, allowing them to make informed decisions when planning or responding to new emergencies. These documents not only preserve critical knowledge but also inspire confidence in handling complex situations by illustrating successful strategies previously employed.

To maximize the usability of this repository, clear indexing and keyword tagging should be implemented. Ease of access is vital; during an actual crisis or even during routine training exercises, no one wants to sift through stacks of papers or scroll through endless digital documents. By categorizing reports based on type of incident, location, date, and other relevant factors, information can be retrieved quickly and efficiently. For instance, if a fire were to break out, having past incidents of similar nature tagged and at one's fingertips could dramatically enhance response time and effectiveness.

In addition to maintaining written records, fostering open dialogue is equally important. Post-incident debriefings serve as invaluable opportunities for reflection and improvement. They provide a space for individuals to share their experiences, thoughts, and feelings about what transpired. By encouraging these conversations, churches can identify gaps in their current safety plans and work collaboratively to address them. Moreover, debriefings help to solidify a culture of transparency and continuous learning. A team that openly discusses its successes and failures is more likely to grow and develop robust safety measures that truly resonate with everyone involved.

Alongside these discussions, it's beneficial to create case studies from significant events. These case studies act as practical learning tools, offering detailed analyses of particular incidents, including what went right, what went wrong, and why. They transform abstract concepts into tangible examples, showing future leaders different scenarios they might face and the range of possible responses. For instance, a case study on a successful evacuation during extreme weather conditions could provide step-by-step guidance that new leaders can adapt to their situations.

By documenting lessons learned from past incidents, there is a clear guideline on what steps to take when similar circumstances arise. Including these guidelines ensures that leaders don't have to reinvent the wheel each time they're faced with a crisis. Instead, they can rely on well-documented procedures that have been proven effective, minimizing the chaos and uncertainty that often accompany emergencies.

Another aspect worth mentioning is involving the entire community in these processes. While future leaders are the primary beneficiaries of this knowledge base, everyone has a role to play in building and maintaining it. Inviting congregation members to contribute their perspectives and recollections enriches the repository and strengthens communal bonds. When everyone feels invested in the church's safety efforts, there's a shared sense of responsibility and pride in the security and wellbeing of all.

Ultimately, the goal is to create an environment where preparedness is embedded into the fabric of the church community. By cultivating a culture of learning, openness, and collaboration, churches not only protect their current members but also lay a foundation for an enduring legacy of safety. Future leaders will be well-prepared to continue this tradition, equipped with a wealth of knowledge and the confidence to navigate any challenges that may come their way.

Creating a Continuous Improvement Culture

Creating a culture of regular safety evaluation and refinement in the church community is crucial to building a legacy of preparedness. One effective way to achieve this is through consistent training sessions that address diverse emergency scenarios. These sessions not only enhance skill levels but also boost confidence among participants. Imagine gathering on a Saturday afternoon, where church members—young and old alike—participate in drills covering everything from fire evacuation to medical emergencies. These hands-on experiences allow members to practice responses in controlled environments, reducing panic during real incidents.

Training should be varied and comprehensive, considering different types of emergencies. For instance, while many are familiar with basic fire drills, fewer may know the protocols for dealing with severe weather or security threats. By diversifying the training, we ensure that everyone is equipped to handle whatever challenges arise. Rotating topics keeps sessions fresh and engaging, prompting more active participation. Additionally, involving local emergency responders or experts can provide invaluable insights, lending authenticity to exercises and fostering partnerships between the church and community resources.

In parallel with training, establishing feedback mechanisms is essential for ongoing improvement. Encouraging open dialogue after training sessions or real events helps identify what worked well and areas needing enhancement. This could involve simple feedback forms, suggestion boxes, or facilitated group discussions. The key is to create an atmosphere where members feel comfortable sharing their thoughts and ideas. Such feedback is incredibly valuable—it allows leadership to fine-tune safety protocols and adapt training programs to better meet the congregation's needs. Over time, these improvements help cultivate a sense of ownership and collective responsibility for safety among church members.

Next, it's important to integrate safety measures consistently throughout all church activities and event planning. From potlucks to large community gatherings, every event presents unique risks that should be evaluated and addressed. Incorporating safety considerations into early stages of event planning can significantly mitigate potential hazards. For example, ensuring clear exits and accessible first aid stations, and briefing volunteers on emergency procedures can go a long way in ensuring readiness. Regular check-ins and updates at planning meetings keep safety top of mind, reinforcing its importance as a core value of the church's mission.

Equally vital is celebrating successes in safety efforts to maintain enthusiasm and encourage further contributions. Recognizing achievements, whether big or small, can have a powerful impact on morale and motivation. Perhaps it's acknowledging the quick thinking of a staff member who managed a minor medical situation effectively, or highlighting the successful completion of a year without incidents. Celebrations could range from mentions in newsletters to special recognition ceremonies, creating a positive narrative around safety initiatives.

By celebrating victories, we not only affirm the importance of preparedness but also inspire continuous engagement from the community. When people see tangible results of their efforts, they're more likely to stay committed and look for additional ways to contribute. Maintaining a celebratory approach injects energy and positivity into the ongoing journey toward a safer environment.

In summary, fostering regular safety evaluation and refinement requires a multifaceted approach. Consistent training sessions that embrace a wide range of emergency scenarios build foundational skills within the congregation. Establishing robust feedback mechanisms encourages ongoing dialogue and continuous improvement of safety practices. By embedding safety into the fabric of every church activity and recognizing achievements along the way, we not only strengthen preparedness but also reinforce a shared commitment to the wellbeing of the entire community.

Mentoring New Leaders in Preparedness Strategies

Facilitating effective knowledge transfer to new church leaders is an essential part of building a resilient and prepared congregation. One of the most impactful ways to achieve this goal is through mentorship programs. By pairing experienced leaders with emerging ones, we not only create an atmosphere of learning but also ensure that valuable insights and strategies are passed down effectively. These relationships allow experienced leaders to share their wisdom—gleaned from years of managing various situations—and equip new leaders with tried-and-tested strategies for handling the challenges they may face.

Imagine a seasoned leader walking through the experiences that shaped their understanding of safety and preparedness. They might share stories about past emergency responses, providing real-life examples of effective decision-making. Such firsthand accounts help new leaders visualize scenarios they're likely to encounter, making theoretical lessons far more tangible. This approach also fosters a sense of continuity and community, as both mentors and mentees feel connected through shared purpose and mission.

Involving youth and new members in preparedness initiatives can be another powerful strategy. Young people bring fresh energy and innovative thinking, often seeing opportunities and challenges through a different lens. By engaging them in planning and execution, we harness these fresh perspectives, which can lead to creative solutions that might not occur to those who are more set in traditional ways. Youth involvement also ensures that preparedness becomes embedded in the fabric of church life from an early age, cultivating future leaders who are inherently attuned to the importance of safety.

Encouraging young members to take on roles within safety drills or emergency response teams empowers them with responsibility and creates a vested interest in the outcomes of these efforts. For instance, when younger members contribute ideas during planning sessions, they learn about strategic thinking and team collaboration, skills that will serve them well as they transition into leadership roles. Their participation in these activities makes safety and preparedness relevant to them personally, strengthening their commitment to these core values.

Providing comprehensive resources and training is crucial to equipping new leaders with the necessary skills. These resources should include handbooks, online courses, workshops, and possibly even guest speakers from organizations specializing in crisis management or church safety. Training should be continuous and adaptive, reflecting current best practices and addressing new challenges that arise in our ever-changing world.

Think about the impact of a well-organized training workshop where leaders engage in simulated crisis scenarios. These simulations teach quick decision-making, teamwork, and clear communication—essential skills in any emergency. Leaders learn how to apply theoretical knowledge practically, thus building confidence in their ability to manage real-life situations.

Comprehensive resources provide a solid foundation, enabling new leaders to explore topics at their own pace and reference materials as needed. Moving beyond just formal training, creating an environment where informal learning takes place—such as through discussion groups or online forums—can further enhance understanding and readiness.

A critical aspect of maintaining effective knowledge transfer is the regular evaluation of mentoring outcomes. Continuous assessment ensures that the mentoring program remains responsive and relevant. Leaders should periodically review these programs to gauge what's working well and where improvements are needed. Collecting feedback from participants can be invaluable in identifying successes and potential areas for growth.

For example, surveys and debriefings after each mentoring cycle can offer insights into the effectiveness of particular strategies or reveal if adjustments are required to better meet participant needs. Evaluations could encompass assessing whether mentees feel more confident and capable in their roles and whether mentors believe they have had a meaningful impact.

Annual Reflection Reviews and Their Importance

In the journey towards building a legacy of safety and preparedness within a church community, establishing regular, structured reviews is an invaluable strategy. These reviews are not just bureaucratic exercises but are essential in ensuring that learning and improvement become a continuous process.

The first step is to schedule annual reflection reviews. These reviews serve as moments for the entire congregation to pause and evaluate the effectiveness of existing strategies. By setting a recurring date for these reflections, there is a built-in commitment to growth and readiness. The beauty of this process lies in its adaptability; it allows leaders and members alike to learn from the past year's experiences. For instance, if a particular emergency drill didn't go as planned, the review provides an opportunity to dissect what went wrong and brainstorm ways to make it more effective. In doing so, the church can adapt its strategies to better suit future needs, always moving forward with enhanced insight.

Equally important is fostering an inclusive environment where every member feels encouraged to participate in these sessions. The church community is a diverse tapestry, rich with perspectives, each offering unique insights into safety and preparedness. When all voices are invited to contribute, the solutions crafted are comprehensive and reflect the true needs of the congregation. Consider Mrs. Johnson, who may have witnessed firsthand the aftermath of a natural disaster, or young Peter, whose digital savvy could introduce new technologies into the church's preparedness plans. Encouraging such participation ensures that the planning is not only top-down but enriched by grassroots input.

Thorough documentation of these discussions is another cornerstone of the process. It is crucial that all aspects of the reviews are meticulously recorded and stored in a central repository. This practice serves multiple purposes; it creates a living history of the church's efforts while providing a robust reference for when similar scenarios arise in the future. A well-organized archive means that if, say, a severe weather condition is forecasted, leaders can quickly access strategies that were previously discussed for handling such events. Furthermore, this habit of documentation ensures transparency and accountability, reassuring members that their insights are valued and utilized.

Using standard templates during these reviews further streamlines the process. Consistency in how information is collected and presented makes the comparisons between different years straightforward. Imagine looking through several years' worth of reviews and being able to immediately spot trends because the data is uniformly organized. Not only does this ease the burden on those compiling the reports, but it also enables the church leadership to identify areas of progress and aspects needing attention swiftly.

Summary and Reflections

Throughout this chapter, we've highlighted the significance of building a culture of safety and preparedness in church communities. By learning from past incidents, we can create a robust foundation for future leaders. Documenting lessons learned ensures that we're not starting from scratch during emergencies. This ever-evolving knowledge base becomes a central resource, empowering leaders to make informed decisions grounded in real-world experiences. Open conversations after incidents reveal areas for improvement, fostering a transparent environment where everyone feels comfortable sharing insights.

As we move forward, keeping safety at the forefront of every activity remains essential. Regular training sessions equip church members with vital skills to handle various emergency scenarios, ensuring everyone feels ready when challenges arise. Celebrating achievements and involving the whole community reinforces a shared dedication to maintaining a safe environment. Encouraging participation from all generations, including youth, helps embed safety into the church's core values. Together, by continuously evaluating our strategies and supporting new leaders, we are creating a resilient congregation capable of navigating any situation with confidence and unity.

Appendices
- Appendix A: Sample Disaster Response Plan Template
Sample Disaster Response Plan for [Your Church Name]

---

1. Overview of the Church's Disaster Response Plan

Purpose:
To ensure that [Church Name] is prepared for a variety of emergencies and disasters, safeguarding the health, safety, and well-being of its congregation and visitors. This plan outlines the roles and responsibilities of church staff, volunteers, and congregation members in the event of an emergency.

Scope:
This plan applies to natural disasters, health emergencies (e.g., pandemics), civil unrest, man-made disasters, and other crises. It includes preparedness, response, recovery, and continuity of church services.

---

2. Emergency Contacts and Key Personnel

Emergency Response Team:
The church's Disaster Response Team (DRT) is composed of staff and trained volunteers who will coordinate efforts in the event of an emergency.

Position Name Phone Number Email
Incident Commander [Name] [Phone Number] [Email]
Communication Officer [Name] [Phone Number] [Email]
Safety Officer [Name] [Phone Number] [Email]
Volunteer Coordinator [Name] [Phone Number] [Email]
Facilities Manager [Name] [Phone Number] [Email]
Medical Support Officer [Name] [Phone Number] [Email]

---

3. Risk Assessment and Vulnerability Analysis

Location-Specific Risks:

Identify specific risks in the church's geographical area, such as earthquakes, floods, hurricanes, civil unrest, or pandemics.
- Earthquakes: The church is located in a seismic zone.
- Floods: The church is near a floodplain; flash floods are a concern during heavy rains.
- Severe Weather: Tornadoes and thunderstorms are frequent in the summer months.
- Civil Unrest: The church may be at risk during civil disturbances or public protests.
- Health Crises: Preparedness for pandemics or outbreaks (e.g., flu, COVID-19).

---

4. Disaster Preparedness Procedures

Evacuation Procedures:

In the event of an evacuation, the following steps should be followed:

1. Alerting Congregation: Emergency alerts will be sent via phone tree, text messaging, or social media. The communication officer will handle notifications.

2. Evacuation Routes: Clearly marked exits will be used. In case of fire or other immediate dangers, congregants should follow the exit signs and gather at the designated safe assembly area (e.g., parking lot, nearby park).

3. Role of Ushers and Volunteers: Ushers and volunteers will assist with guiding individuals to exits, ensuring that children, elderly, and disabled individuals are safely evacuated.

4. Special Considerations: Ensure that the designated areas for evacuating children, seniors, and people with disabilities are prepared with necessary assistance.

Shelter-In-Place Procedures:

In case of a shelter-in-place situation (e.g., tornado or chemical spill), the following steps should be followed:

1. Alerting Congregation: Announcement via loudspeaker, text alerts, and social media to inform all present to shelter indoors.
2. Safe Areas: The designated safe areas in the church facility (e.g., basement, interior rooms with no windows) will be used.
3. First Aid and Medical Care: The medical officer will set up a temporary first-aid station if needed. Supplies and trained personnel should be available.

---

5. Communication Plan

Communication Strategy:

The church will use the following methods to communicate during an emergency:

- Primary Communication Method: Text messages, phone tree, social media posts, and email to keep the congregation informed.
- Secondary Communication Method: Public announcement system, handheld radios, or runners (volunteers) for on-site communication.
- External Communication: The church will coordinate with local authorities, first responders, and neighboring churches for mutual support.

Communication Officer's Responsibilities:

- Monitor weather and emergency alerts.
- Send emergency notifications to church members.
- Keep the congregation updated on the status of the situation and recovery efforts.
- Ensure that any required evacuations or shelter-in-place orders are communicated clearly and promptly.

---

6. Emergency Supplies and Equipment

Essential Emergency Supplies:

- Water and Non-Perishable Food: At least a 72-hour supply for all members.

- First Aid Kits: Easily accessible, stocked with bandages, antiseptics, medications, etc.
- Flashlights and Batteries: Backup light sources for power outages.
- Blankets and Sleeping Bags: In case sheltering overnight is necessary.
- Medical Supplies: Including first-aid kits, defibrillators (AEDs), and any medications required for vulnerable congregants.
- Backup Power: Generators to power essential church systems (lights, medical equipment).
- Personal Protective Equipment (PPE): Face masks, gloves, hand sanitizers, etc., especially in cases of infectious disease outbreaks.

Facilities Manager's Responsibilities:
- Ensure that all emergency supplies are stored in accessible locations.
- Check expiration dates and replace supplies regularly.
- Verify the functioning of all emergency equipment (e.g., generators, PA systems).

---

7. Roles and Responsibilities of Staff and Volunteers
- Incident Commander: Leads the response efforts, makes decisions on evacuation, sheltering, and communication.
- Safety Officer: Oversees the safety of all individuals, manages evacuation procedures, and ensures the building is secure.
- Volunteer Coordinator: Manages volunteer efforts, assigns roles (e.g., guiding congregants, preparing supplies).
- Medical Support Officer: Provides first aid, triage, and medical care.
- Communication Officer: Manages all communication, including internal and external alerts.
- Facilities Manager: Ensures that the building is safe, that emergency exits are clear, and that supplies are available.

---

8. Post-Disaster Recovery and Continuity of Operations
Recovery Phase:
- Assessment: After a disaster, the response team will assess the damage to the building, equipment, and the congregation's well-being.
- Continuing Communication: The communication officer will keep the congregation updated on the church's status, any damage, and ongoing recovery efforts.
- Mental Health Support: The church will provide counseling and support groups for affected individuals.
- Reopening Services: The church will assess when it is safe to reopen and resume services. The safety of congregants is the priority.

Continuity of Operations:
- Remote Services: In the event of a prolonged closure, services may continue via online streaming or recorded messages.
- Financial Continuity: The church will continue its financial operations through online giving platforms to support recovery efforts.

---

9. Review and Testing of the Disaster Plan
- Annual Drills: The Disaster Response Team will conduct annual drills to practice evacuation, sheltering, and communication procedures.
- Plan Review: This plan will be reviewed annually and updated based on changes in church structure, local risks, and feedback from drills.
- Feedback: After each disaster or drill, feedback will be collected from staff, volunteers, and congregants to identify areas of improvement.

---

10. Conclusion and Commitment to Preparedness
[Church Name] is committed to being a safe, resilient place for our congregation and community. By working together and being proactive, we can ensure that our church is prepared for any disaster and can continue to serve as a place of refuge and support during times of crisis.

- Appendix B: Emergency Supply Checklist
Emergency Supply Checklist for [Church Name] (100 People)

---

1. Water and Food Supplies
- Water: At least 1 gallon of water per person per day for 3 days (300 gallons total).
- Non-perishable food: Enough to feed 100 people for 3 days (canned goods, granola bars, dried fruits, crackers, etc.).
o Canned beans, vegetables, soups, tuna, etc. (minimum 300 cans)
o Ready-to-eat meals (MREs) or freeze-dried food (minimum 300 servings)
o Protein bars and snacks (minimum 100 servings)
- Manual can opener: 2 heavy-duty manual can openers.
- Cooking equipment: Portable stoves or grills, with fuel (propane or charcoal), and cookware.
- Utensils, plates, and cups: Disposable plates, cups, and utensils (100 sets).

---

2. First Aid and Medical Supplies
- First-aid kits: At least 2 fully stocked kits with:
o Bandages (various sizes)
o Gauze, medical tape, and antiseptic wipes
o Tweezers, scissors, and gloves
o Thermometers, pain relievers (Tylenol, Advil)
o Antihistamines (Benadryl)
o Alcohol pads, burn ointment, and eye wash
o Adhesive bandages, butterfly closures, and sterile pads
- Personal protective equipment (PPE):
o 200 face masks (N95 or surgical)
o 100 pairs of gloves
o 100 disposable gowns or ponchos
o 20 face shields

- Prescription medications: A 3-day supply of any critical medications (especially for elderly members or those with chronic conditions).
- Medical supplies:
  o 2 automatic external defibrillators (AEDs)
  o Blood pressure cuffs, stethoscopes
  o Instant cold packs and hot packs
- Sanitation items: Hand sanitizers (10 bottles), disinfecting wipes (5 containers).

---

3. Shelter and Comfort Items
- Blankets and sleeping bags: At least 100 blankets or sleeping bags.
- Tents: 2 large tents or pop-up shelters for emergency sheltering (can accommodate 10-20 people per tent).
- Mattresses or pads: 50 air mattresses or sleeping pads.
- Cushions/pillows: 50 pillows (optional, but can increase comfort during long stays).
- Tarps: 10 large tarps (for covering windows, shelters, or vehicles).

---

4. Communication Tools
- Two-way radios: At least 10 two-way radios (walkie-talkies) for communication between staff and volunteers.
- Cell phone chargers: 10 portable power banks for charging mobile phones and communication devices.
- Emergency whistle: 20 loud whistles to signal for attention.
- Batteries: A 3-day supply of batteries for flashlights, radios, and other equipment (100 batteries of each size needed).

---

5. Lighting and Power Supplies
- Flashlights: At least 10 LED flashlights with extra batteries.
- Lanterns: 5 battery-powered or solar lanterns for larger area lighting.

- Generator: 1 portable generator (capable of powering essential systems for several hours) with 5 gallons of fuel.
- Solar chargers: 5 solar-powered battery chargers for backup power.

---

6. Hygiene and Sanitation
- Toiletries:
o 10 rolls of toilet paper (per day for 3 days: 30 rolls)
o 5 bars of soap
o 5 bottles of hand sanitizer
o Toothbrushes and toothpaste (100 sets)
- Waste disposal:
o 10 large trash bags (for general waste)
o 10 biohazard waste bags (for medical waste)
- Sanitation stations: Portable hand-washing stations (with water storage if no running water is available).
- Feminine hygiene products: 100 packets of sanitary pads, tampons, etc.

---

7. Fire and Safety Equipment
- Fire extinguishers: At least 4 fire extinguishers (one for each major area of the church).
- Smoke detectors: 10 smoke detectors with extra batteries.
- Emergency exit signs: 5 emergency exit lights with battery backup.

---

8. Evacuation and Signage
- Exit signs: Ensure all exit signs are clearly visible, with backup power in case of electricity failure.
- Evacuation maps: 10 printed evacuation maps showing primary and secondary exits, and assembly areas.
- Megaphone: 1 battery-powered megaphone for mass communication during an evacuation.

---

9. Personal and Family Emergency Kits
- Individual emergency kits (for each family or individual attending):
  o 1 small first-aid kit (band-aids, antiseptic wipes, pain relief)
  o 1 water bottle
  o 1 snack pack (granola bar, nuts, dried fruits)
  o 1 flashlight with extra batteries
  o 1 small hygiene kit (toothbrush, hand sanitizer, wipes)

---

10. Miscellaneous
- Backup documentation: Digital and hard copies of emergency contacts, insurance policies, important church documents, and evacuation plans.
- Cash: A small emergency fund (preferably in cash) for emergency purchases when card machines may not be working.
- Entertainment: Games or activities for children (books, small toys, board games, etc.).

Total Emergency Supplies Overview
Item Quantity Purpose
Water 300 gallons Hydration for 100 people for 3 days
Non-perishable food 300 servings Emergency nutrition for 100 people for 3 days
First Aid Kits 2 Medical supplies for emergencies
Personal protective equipment 100+ masks, gloves, etc. Health protection for all congregants
Blankets/Sleeping bags 100 blankets Shelter and warmth
Two-way radios 10 Communication during evacuation and emergency response
Flashlights/Lanterns 15 Lighting for power outages
Toiletries Sufficient supply Hygiene maintenance during emergencies

Fire extinguishers 4 Fire safety
Generator and Fuel 1 generator Power backup for essential services

---

Important Notes

• Regularly Rotate Supplies: Ensure that food, water, and medical supplies are rotated every 6 months to maintain freshness and effectiveness.

• Train Volunteers: Designate key volunteers for handling supplies, guiding evacuations, and first-aid assistance.

• Review and Update Plan: Annually review the checklist and update any expired or damaged items.

By ensuring that these essential supplies are available and easily accessible, your church will be well-prepared to respond to a variety of emergency situations and provide for the safety and well-being of your congregation during times of crisis.

- Appendix C: Resources for Mental Health Support in Disasters

Resources for mental health support in disasters

- Disaster Distress Helpline

Call 1-800-985-5990 or text "TalkWithUs" to 66746 for immediate help

- American Academy of Experts in Traumatic Stress

A network of professionals who work to improve interventions for trauma survivors

- American Psychological Association

Provides tools and practices to help people and communities build resilience

- Crisis Counseling Assistance and Training Program (CCP)

Helps individuals and communities recover from disasters through community outreach and access to mental health services

- Disaster Behavioral Health

Provides mental health, substance abuse, and stress management services to disaster survivors and responders

Other resources Iowa Disaster Behavioral Health Response Team, American Red Cross, and FEMA.gov.

- Appendix D: Contact Information for Local and National Disaster Relief Organizations

To contact a national disaster relief organization, you can reach the Federal Emergency Management Agency (FEMA) helpline at 1-800-621-FEMA (3362). You can also access disaster assistance information online at DisasterAssistance.gov.

Key points about contacting FEMA:
- General questions: Call 1-800-621-3362
- Website: DisasterAssistance.gov
- For hearing/speech impaired: Call 1-800-462-7585

Other relevant organizations:
- American Red Cross: Contact for general disaster relief services
- Local Emergency Management Agency: Check with your state or local government for contact details

About the Author

M.Ray Davis has been a prepper since 1998, when the Y2K scare first sparked his interest in self-reliance. While the world didn't end that New Year's Eve, he quickly realized that real-world events—storms, power outages, job loss, illness—were more than enough reason to build a preparedness lifestyle.

By 2009, he had earned his Amateur Radio license, discovering what would become a lifelong passion for radio communications. A decade later, he upgraded to General class, opening the door to worldwide contacts and the ability to connect with people across the globe.

A true believer in practical prepping, M.Ray Davis has spent more than two decades combining food, water, shelter, and communications into a sustainable lifestyle—without panic, without hype. His mission is to help others do the same: prepare for the everyday disruptions that really happen, and build the skills to face them with confidence.

When he's not on the air or testing gear in the field, you'll find him writing, podcasting, and teaching others how to step into preparedness with common sense and a little bit of humor.

www.ingramcontent.com/pod-product-compliance
Lightning Source LLC
Chambersburg PA
CBHW070325100426
42743CB00011B/2561